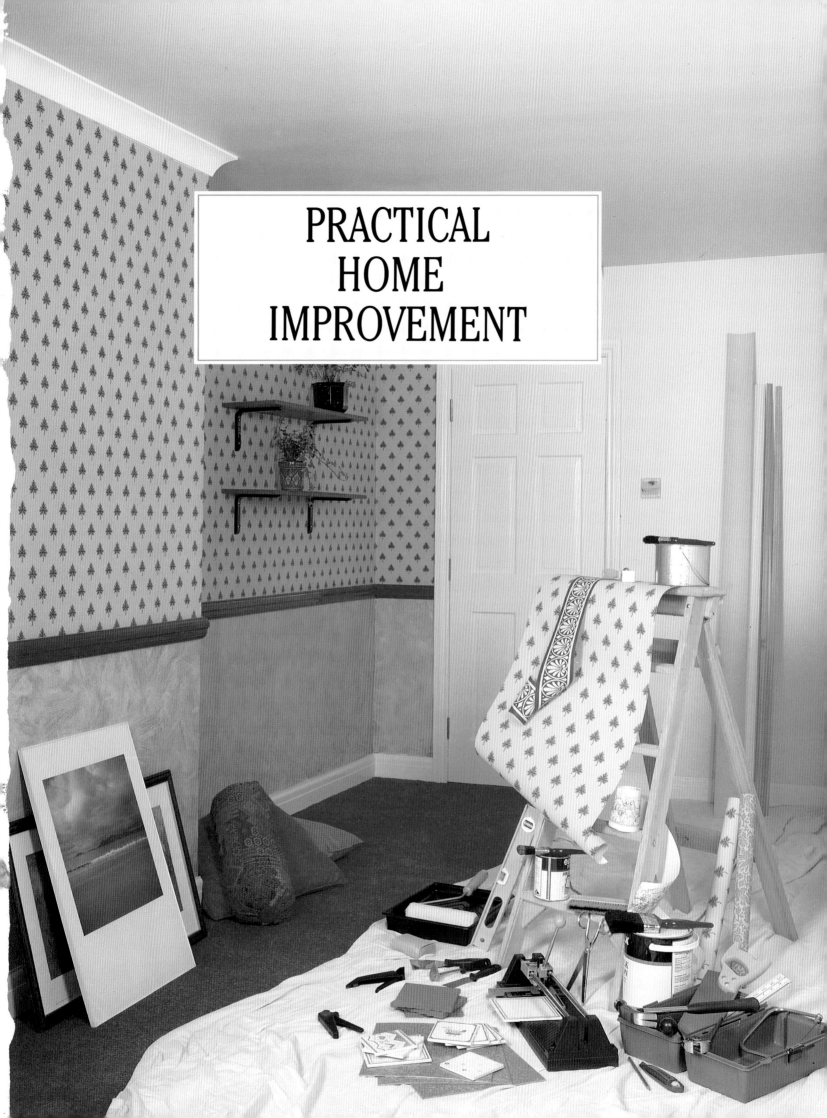

PRACTICAL
HOME
IMPROVEMENT

PRACTICAL HOME IMPROVEMENT

MIKE LAWRENCE

READ ON PUBLICATIONS

© Anness Publishing Limited 1995

Lorenz Books is an imprint of
Anness Publishing Limited
1 Boundary Row
London SE1 8HP

This edition published in 1995 by
Read On Publications Inc.
100 The East Mall,
Unit 5,
Toronto, Ontario
M825X2, Canada
Phone: (416) 503-3444
Fax: (416) 503-9386

Reprinted in 1995

ISBN 1 85967 045 8
A CIP catalogue record for this book
is available from the British Library.

Publisher Joanna Lorenz
Senior Editor Judith Simons
Designer Michael Morey
Photographer John Freeman
Illustrator Andrew Green

Typeset by MC Typeset Limited, Rochester, Kent
Printed and bound in Singapore
by Star Standard Industries

PUBLISHER'S NOTE

The author and publishers have made every effort to ensure that all instructions
contained within this book are accurate and safe, and cannot accept liability for
any resulting injury, damage or loss to persons or property however it may arise.
If in any doubt as to the correct procedure to follow for any home improvements
task, seek professional advice.

CONTENTS

INTRODUCTION

Every home needs repainting, updating or repair work
to keep it looking fresh, stylish and in good
condition. Whether you have a new house in need of
additional features and fittings, an old property requiring
a major overhaul, or simply want to refresh an outmoded
decorating scheme, this book will provide all the
guidance, expertise and know-how needed for complete
success and perfect results every time.

This invaluable book is completely practical, covering
Painting, Paperhanging, Tiling, Laying Floor Coverings,
Features and Fittings, and closing with a section
on the everyday Maintenance and Repairs that
every householder has to face from time to time.

Each chapter contains all the instructive and problem-solving information you need, and a wide range of step-by-step techniques and projects, as well as full information on the tools that will be used. There is advice on the types of materials available, the necessary tools and equipment, and plenty of professional hints and tips to ensure that every technique is accessible and easy to follow. Full-colour step-by-step photographs appear throughout the book, plus explanatory illustrations, useful charts, and a wealth of practical advice on creating the ideal interior without spending a fortune.

Aimed at everyone from the novice home decorator to the experienced enthusiast, **Practical Home Improvement** covers all the different areas of practical do-it-yourself required to make the very best of your home.

PAINTING

Painting walls, woodwork and other surfaces is, so all the surveys reveal, by far the most popular do-it-yourself job. Modern paints and improvements in the design and manufacture of decorating tools have certainly made the task less arduous than it was in the days of traditional oil-bound paints and distemper, and have also made it easier for the amateur decorator to get professional-looking results.

One major shift in paint technology is the trend away from using solvent-based varnishes and paints for wood, towards water-based products which do not give off harmful vapours as they dry. Water-based finishes are not as durable as solvent-based ones, but are no longer as far behind them in performance terms as they once were, and they have other advantages such as faster drying times, virtually no smell and easier cleaning of brushes, rollers and pads. It is therefore likely that their use in the home will become much more widespread.

No amount of clever technology can eliminate the need for proper preparation of the surfaces to be decorated, even though this part of the job is far less enjoyable and often more time-consuming than the actual painting. In many cases it involves little more than washing the surface down, but sometimes more thorough preparation will be called for.

This chapter describes, stage by stage, how to prepare surfaces for redecoration and how to apply the new finish – especially to the more awkward surfaces such as windows and panelled doors – for highly professional results.

PAINTING TOOLS AND EQUIPMENT

Two groups of tools are needed, one for preparing the surface and one for actually putting the paint on. For a masonry wall, the minimum preparation is to wash down any previously painted surface. This calls for a bucket, sponges and cloths, strong household detergent or sugar soap (all-purpose cleaner), and rubber gloves to protect the hands.

If the washed-down surface has a high-gloss finish, or feels rough to the touch, use fine abrasive paper (sandpaper) and a sanding block to smooth it down. Wet-and-dry (silicon carbide) paper, used wet, is best for sanding down existing paintwork; rinse off the resulting fine slurry of paint with water afterwards. Use ordinary abrasive paper for bare wood.

Defects in the surface need filling. Use a traditional cellulose filler (spackle) for small cracks, chips and other surface blemishes, and an expanding filler foam which can be shaped and sanded when hard for larger defects. To apply filler paste use a filling knife (putty knife).

To strip existing paintwork, use either a heat gun – easier to control and much safer to use than a blowtorch – or a chemical paint remover, plus scrapers of various shapes to remove the softened paint. For removing wall coverings in order to apply a painted wall or ceiling finish, a steam wallpaper stripper will be invaluable. The small all-in-one strippers which resemble a large steam iron are the easiest type to use.

Painting tools

The paintbrush is still the favourite tool for applying paint to walls, ceilings, woodwork and metalwork around the house. Most are made with natural bristle, held in a metal ferrule which is attached to a wooden or plastic handle, but there are also brushes with synthetic fibre bristles which are sometimes recommended for applying water-based (latex) paints.

Brushes come in widths from 12 mm (½ in) up to 150 mm (6 in). The smallest sizes are used for fiddly jobs such as painting glazing bars (muntins), while the widest are ideal for flat uninterrupted wall and ceiling surfaces. However, a wide brush can be tiring to use, especially with solvent-based (oil) paints. There are also long-handled

PREPARATION EQUIPMENT

The following tools and equipment are the general items needed to prepare for repainting: steam wallpaper stripper (**1**), liquid paint remover (**2**), paste paint remover (**3**), cellulose filler (spackle) (**4**), expanding filler foam (**5**), rubber gloves (**6**), bucket (**7**), sugar soap (all-purpose cleaner) (**8**), sponge (**9**), cloth (**10**), spray gun (**11**), abrasive paper (sandpaper) (**12**), sanding block (**13**), shavehooks (triangular scrapers) (**14**), scrapers (**15**), heat gun and attachments (a directional nozzle and two integral scrapers) (**16**).

brushes with angled heads for painting behind radiators, and narrow brushes called *cutting-in* (sash) brushes, which have the bristle tips cut off at an angle for painting into internal angles. For the best results, buy good-quality brushes and look after them, rather than buy cheap ones and throw them away after finishing the job.

Paint rollers are used mainly for painting walls and ceilings with water-based paints, although they can be used with solvent-based types too. They consist of a metal roller cage mounted on a handle, plus a hollow sleeve that fits onto the cage and actually applies the paint. Some can be fitted with an extension pole, which is useful if there are high ceilings or stairwells to paint. Most rollers are 180 mm (7 in) wide;

larger sizes are available, but can be harder to 'drive'. There are also slim mini-rollers for painting awkward-to-reach areas such as walls behind radiators. For any type, a roller tray is used to load paint onto the sleeve. Solid water-based paint is sold in its own tray.

The sleeves are waterproof tubes with a layer of foam plastic or cloth stuck to the outside. The second type may be made from natural or synthetic fibre, and have a short, medium or long pile. Choose the pile length to match the surface being painted: short for flat surfaces, medium for those with a slight texture and long for heavily embossed or sculpted surfaces.

Paint pads are squares or rectangles of short-pile cloth stuck to a foam backing

and mounted on a plastic or metal handle. The pad is dipped in a shallow container, or loaded from a special paint container with a roller feed, and then drawn across the surface. Pads come in a range of sizes.

Paint and varnish are also sold in *aerosol* form. This is ideal for small areas or fiddly materials such as wickerwork, but too expensive to use on large areas.

Lastly, do not forget the decorating sundries. A *paint kettle* is needed for decanting the paint and straining out any foreign bodies. Hand-held *paint masks* or *masking tape* are invaluable aids to getting straight edges and keeping paint off adjacent surfaces. Above all, remember to provide *dust sheets* (drop cloths), which perform better than plastic sheets.

PAINTING EQUIPMENT

This selection of equipment includes: brushes in various sizes (**1**), aerosol paint (**2**), long-handled brush for use behind radiators (**3**), hand-held skirting (baseboard) masks (**4**), slimline mini-roller (**5**), roller extension pole (**6**), a full-sized roller with short-pile sleeve and roller tray (**7**), dust sheet (drop cloth) (**8**), white spirit (paint thinner) (**9**), long pile and textured roller sleeves (**10**), paint shield (**11**), masking tape (**12**), paint kettle (**13**), paint pads in various sizes and shapes (**14**), paint-loading containers for paint pads (**15**).

PREPARING SURFACES FOR PAINTING

Modern paints have excellent adhesion and covering power, but to get the best performance from them they must be given a good start by preparing the surface thoroughly.

Wash surfaces, which have previously been painted, using a solution of strong household detergent or sugar soap (all-purpose cleaner). Rinse them very thoroughly with clean water, and allow them to dry completely before starting repainting.

Remove areas of flaking paint with a scraper or filling knife (putty knife), and then either touch in the bare area with more paint or fill it flush with the surrounding paint film by using fine filler (spackle). Sand this smooth when it has hardened.

If the surface shows signs of mildew growth due to persistent condensation, wipe it over with household bleach, or refrigerator cleaner containing a fungicide, to kill off the spores. Wash down the surface with detergent and rinse thoroughly.

If knots are showing through on painted woodwork, sand the paint film back to bare wood and apply knotting (shellac) to the knot, then prime and undercoat to bring the new paint film level with the surrounding paintwork. Sand between coats. Resinous knots may produce stains which can only be prevented by drying the knot out with a blowtorch.

PREPARING PAINTED WOODWORK

1 Use fine-grade abrasive paper (sandpaper) wrapped around a sanding block to remove 'nibs' from the paint surface and to key the paint film ready for repainting.

2 Wash the surface down with detergent or sugar soap (all-purpose cleaner) to remove dirt, grease, finger marks and the dust from sanding it. Rinse with clean water, ensuring that no detergent residue is left as this will inhibit the new paint film.

3 Use a proprietary tack rag or a clean cloth moistened with white spirit (paint thinner) to remove dust from recessed mouldings and other awkward corners.

FILLING DEFECTS IN WOOD

1 Fill splits and dents in wood using filler (spackle) on painted surfaces, and tinted wood stopper (patcher) on new or stripped wood that will be varnished.

2 Use the corner of a filling knife (putty knife), or even a finger, to work the filler into recesses and other awkward-to-reach places. Smooth off excess filler before it dries.

3 When the filler or wood stopper has hardened completely, use abrasive paper (sandpaper) wrapped around a sanding block to sand the repair down flush.

FILLING CRACKS IN PLASTER

1 Use the corner of a filling knife (putty knife) to rake out loose material along the line of the crack, and to undercut the edges slightly so that the filler has a better grip.

2 Brush out dust and debris from the crack, using an old paintbrush. Alternatively, use the crevice nozzle attachment of a vacuum cleaner.

3 Dampen the surrounding plaster with water from a garden spray gun to prevent it from drying out the filler too quickly and causing it to crack.

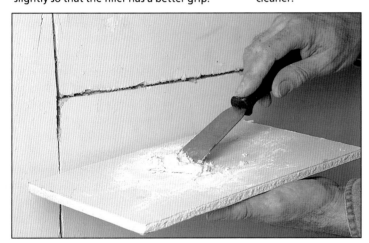

4 Mix up some filler on a plasterer's hawk (mortarboard) or a board offcut to a firm consistency. Alternatively, use ready-mixed filler or wallboard compound.

5 Use a filling knife to press the filler well into the crack, drawing the blade across it and then along it. Aim to leave the repair slightly proud.

DEALING WITH STAINS

If ceilings have been stained by plumbing leaks, seal the affected area with a proprietary aerosol stain sealer to prevent the stain from showing through the new paint film. Alternatively, paint the affected area with white gloss (oil) paint – it will seal just as well and is usually already on hand. It can be overpainted with water-based (latex) paint.

6 When the filler has hardened, use fine-grade abrasive paper (sandpaper) wrapped around a sanding block to smooth the repair flush with the surrounding wall.

STRIPPING PAINT

Every time a surface is repainted, this adds a little more thickness to the paint layer. It does not matter much on wall or ceiling surfaces, but on woodwork (and, to a lesser extent, on metalwork) this build-up of successive layers of paint can eventually lead to the clogging of detail on mouldings. More importantly, moving parts such as doors and windows start to bind and catch against their frames. If this happens, it is time to strip off the paint back to bare wood and build up a new paint system from scratch.

It may also be necessary to strip an old paint finish if it is in such poor condition – from physical damage, for example – that repainting will no longer cover up the faults adequately.

There are two methods of removing paint from wood and metal surfaces. The first is using *heat*, traditionally from a blowtorch but nowadays more often an electric heat gun. The second is to use a *chemical paint remover*, which contains either dimethylene chloride or caustic soda. Heat works well on wood, but may scorch the surface and can crack the glass in windows; it is less successful on metal because the material conducts heat away as it is applied. Chemicals work well on all surfaces, but need handling with care; always follow the manufacturer's instructions to the letter.

HOMEMADE PASTE REMOVER

Add caustic soda to water until no more will dissolve. Thicken to a paste with oatmeal and use as for proprietary paste remover. Be particularly careful when using this corrosive solution. If it splashes on the skin, rinse at once with plenty of cold water.

USING A HEAT GUN

1 Play the air stream from the heat gun over the surface to soften the paint film. Scrape it off as it bubbles up, and deposit the hot scrapings in an old metal container.

2 Use a shavehook (triangular scraper) instead of a flat scraper to remove the paint from mouldings. Take care not to scorch the wood if it is to be varnished afterwards.

3 Remove any remnants of paint from the wood surface with wire wool soaked in white spirit (paint thinner), working along the direction of the grain.

4 Use a hand vacuum cleaner to remove any remaining loose particles of paint from the crevices in mouldings and from any other inaccessible areas.

5 Sand the surface of the wood lightly to remove any raised fibres or rough patches, then wipe it over with a clean cloth moistened with white spirit.

6 Seal the resin in any exposed knots by brushing on a coat of liquid knotting (shellac). Leave this to dry thoroughly before priming the wood.

7 Apply a coat of either wood primer or a combined primer/undercoat to the stripped wood surface to provide optimum adhesion for the subsequent top coats.

USING LIQUID REMOVER

1 Wear rubber gloves and old clothing. Decant the liquid into a polythene (polyethylene) container or an old can, then brush it onto the surface you want to strip. Leave it until the paint film bubbles up.

2 Use a flat scraper or shavehook (triangular scraper) as appropriate to remove the softened paint. Deposit the scrapings safely in an old container.

3 Neutralize the stripper by washing the surface down with water or white spirit (paint thinner), as recommended by the manufacturer. Leave it to dry.

USING PASTE REMOVER

1 Paste removers are especially good for removing paint from intricate mouldings because they dry very slowly. Apply the paste liberally to the surface.

2 Give the paste plenty of time to work, especially on thick paint layers. Then scrape it off and wash down the surface with plenty of water to neutralize the chemical.

P A I N T I N G

The paintbrush is the most versatile and therefore the most widely used tool for applying paint. Choose the brush size to match the surface being painted. For example, for painting glazing bars (muntins) on windows or narrow mouldings on a door, use a slim brush – or perhaps a cutting-in (sash) brush if painting up to an adjacent unpainted surface such as glass where a neat edge to the paint film is needed. For

expansive, flat areas select a larger brush for quick coverage. Remember that the largest wall brushes can be tiring to use, especially with solvent-based (oil) paints.

Get rid of any loose bristles in a new brush by flicking it vigorously across the palm of the hand before using it for the first time. Wash previously used brushes that have been stored unwrapped to remove any dust or other debris from

the bristles, and leave them to dry out again before using them to apply a solvent-based paint.

Always check that the metal ferrule is securely attached to the brush handle, and hammer in any projecting nails or staples. Check too that the ferrule is free from rust which could discolour the paint. To remove rust use either wire wool or abrasive paper (sandpaper).

PREPARING THE PAINT

1 Wipe the lid first to remove any dust. Then prise it off with a wide lever such as the thicker edge of a table knife to avoid damage to the lip.

2 Decant some paint into a clean metal or plastic paint kettle, or small bucket. This is easier to handle than a full container, especially one without a handle.

3 Remove any paint skin from partly used containers. Then strain the paint into the paint kettle through a piece of old stocking or tights (pantyhose), or cheesecloth.

HOLDING THE BRUSH

1 Before using a new brush, work it vigorously backwards and forwards across the palm of the hand to remove any loose bristles. Wash stored brushes.

2 The best control of a small or medium-sized brush is achieved by holding it with the fingers and thumb on the ferrule, rather than on the handle.

3 Wide wall brushes can be tiring to use, and it is usually more comfortable to grip the brush by the handle rather than by the ferrule.

USING A BRUSH

1 To load the brush with paint, dip it into the paint to about a third of the bristle depth. An overloaded brush will cause drips, and paint will run down the brush handle.

2 Tie a length of string or wire across the mouth of the paint kettle between the handle supports, and use it to scrape excess paint from the bristles.

3 Apply the paint to the wood in long, sweeping strokes, brushing the paint out along the grain direction until the brush begins to run dry.

4 Load up the brush with more paint and apply it to the next area. Blend the two together with short, light strokes, again along the grain direction.

5 Repeat this process while working across the area, blending the edges of adjacent areas together with light brushstrokes to avoid leaving a visible join.

6 At edges and external corners, let the brush run off the edge to avoid a build-up of paint on the corner. Repeat the process for the opposite edge.

Paint rollers are generally used to apply water-based (latex) paints to large, flat areas such as walls and ceilings. Choose a sleeve with a short pile for painting plaster, a medium pile for painting embossed or textured wall coverings, and a long pile for deeply sculpted surfaces such as those created with textured finishes (texture paints). Rollers can also apply solvent-based (oil) paint to flat surfaces such as flush doors, but tend to leave a distinctive 'orange peel' texture rather than the smooth finish left by a paintbrush.

There are some drawbacks with paint rollers: they cannot paint right up to internal corners or wall/ceiling angles, so these need to be painted first with a brush or pad. They can also splash if 'driven' too fast, and the sleeves take a lot of time and effort to clean thoroughly, especially if they have been used for a long period and there is dried paint in the pile. Repeated cleaning eventually causes the sleeve to peel from its core.

People either love or loathe paint pads. They tend to apply less paint per coat than either a brush or a roller, so an additional coat may be needed in some circumstances, but they make it easy to apply paint smoothly and evenly with no risk of brush marks.

USING A ROLLER

1 Select a sleeve with the required fibre type and pile length, and slide it onto the sprung metal cage until it meets the stop next to the handle.

2 Decant some paint (previously strained if from an old can) into the roller tray until the paint level just laps up the sloping section.

3 Brush a band of paint about 50 mm (2 in) wide into internal corners and wall/ceiling angles, around doors and windows, and above skirtings (baseboards).

4 Load the roller sleeve with paint by running it down the sloping section into the paint. Then roll it up and down the slope to remove the excess.

5 Start applying the paint in a series of overlapping diagonal strokes to ensure complete coverage of the surface. Continue until the sleeve runs dry.

6 Reload the sleeve and tackle the next section in the same way. Finish off by blending the areas together, working parallel to corners and edges.

USING A PAINT PAD

1 Pour some paint into the special applicator tray. Then load the pad by running it backwards and forwards over the ridged loading roller.

2 On walls, apply the paint in a series of overlapping parallel bands. Use a small pad or a special edging pad (see step 4) to paint right up to corners or angles.

3 Use smaller pads for painting narrow areas such as mouldings on doors or glazing bars (muntins) on windows, brushing out the paint along the direction of the grain.

4 Special edging pads are designed for painting right up to internal angles, and have small wheels which guide the pad along the adjacent surface as you work.

USING AEROSOL PAINT

Aerosol paints and varnishes are ideal for hard-to-decorate surfaces such as wickerwork. Always follow the maker's instructions when using them.

5 Some larger pads can be fitted to an extension pole to make it easier to paint ceilings and high walls. Make sure the pad is attached securely.

PAINTING WALLS AND CEILINGS

Paint is a popular decorative finish for walls and ceilings because it is quick and easy to apply, offers a huge range of colours and is relatively inexpensive compared with rival products such as wall coverings. It can be used over plain plaster, or can be applied over embossed relief wall coverings and textured finishes.

Before starting painting, clear the room and prepare the surfaces. Start by taking down curtains and blinds (drapes and shades). Remove furniture to another room if possible, or else group it in the middle of the room and cover it with clear plastic sheeting. Take down lampshades and pendant light fittings (after turning off the power supply). Unscrew wall-mounted fittings and remove the hardware from doors and windows if they are being repainted at the same time.

Protect surfaces not being repainted, such as wall switches and socket outlets (receptacles), with masking tape. Finally, cover the floor with dust sheets (drop cloths), which will absorb paint splashes; vacuum-clean surfaces such as window sills, picture rails and skirtings (baseboards) where dust can settle, and turn off forced-air heating so that dust is not recirculated into the room.

Access equipment

Normally most of the surfaces to be painted can be reached from a standing or a kneeling position, but for ceilings, the tops of room walls and the upper reaches of stairwells some access equipment is needed. A simple stepladder, ideally with a top platform big enough to support a paint kettle or roller tray, will be adequate for painting walls and ceilings.

PAINTING WALLS AND CEILINGS

Paint walls and ceilings in a series of overlapping bands. Start painting the ceiling next to the window wall so that reflected light on the wet paint shows whether coverage is even. On walls, right-handed people should work from right to left, and left-handed people the other way.

For stairwells, use steps or ladder sections plus secured scaffold boards or the components of a slot-together access tower to set up a work platform that allows you to get to all the surfaces without over-reaching.

Texture paints

Texture paints are water-based (latex) paints thickened with added fillers. Once the paint has been applied to the decorating surface, a range of three-dimensional effects can be created using various patterning or texturing techniques. These paints are ideal for covering up surfaces in poor condition. Most are white, but they can be overpainted with ordinary water-based paint for a coloured effect. Avoid using them in kitchens – the textured surface will trap dirt and grease which is difficult to clean.

PAINT COVERAGE

Paint coverage depends on several factors, including the roughness and porosity of the surface to which it is being applied and the thickness of the coating. For example, the first coat of paint will soak into new plaster, so the coverage will be less than is achieved with subsequent coats. Similarly, a textured surface will hold more paint than a smooth one, again reducing the paint coverage.

The figures given here are intended as a rough guide only. Always check the manufacturer's coverage figure on the container, and use that plus the area to be painted to work out how much paint is required.

ESTIMATING QUANTITIES

Paint type	Sq m per litre	Sq ft per gallon
Liquid gloss (oil) paint	16	650
Non-drip gloss paint	13	530
Eggshell	12	490
Matt (flat) water-based (latex) paint	15	610
Silk (satin) water-based paint	14	570
Non-drip water-based paint	12	490
Undercoat	11	450
Wood primer	12	490
Metal primer	10	410
Varnish	15–20	610–820

USING TEXTURE PAINT

1 Start applying the paint to the wall or ceiling surface in a series of overlapping random strokes, recharging the roller or brush at intervals.

2 When an area of about 1 sq m (11 sq ft) is covered, go over the whole area with a series of parallel roller/brush strokes for an even surface texture.

3 Give the textured finish the look of tree bark by drawing a flat-bladed scraper or similar edged tool over the surface to flatten off the high spots.

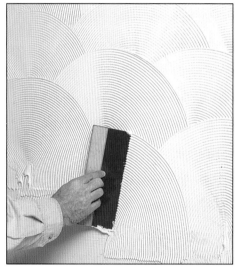

4 Use a texturing comb to create overlapping swirls, working across the area. Practise the effect on paint applied to a piece of heavy cardboard first.

5 Twist a sponge before pulling it away from the wall surface to create a series of small, overlapping swirls in the paint finish. Rinse the sponge regularly.

6 You can buy patterning roller sleeves in a range of different designs for use with texture paints. This one creates a regular diamond pattern.

7 This patterning sleeve gives a random streaked effect when rolled down the wall. Apply the texture paint with a brush first if using a patterning sleeve.

PAINTING DOORS

The main problem with painting doors – or indeed any woodwork with a large surface area – involves keeping what professional decorators call a *wet edge*. Obviously the door has to be painted bit by bit, and if the edge of one area begins to dry before this is joined up to the next area, the join will show when the paint dries completely.

The secret of success is to work in a sequence, as shown in the accompanying drawings of flush and panelled doors, and to complete the job in one continuous operation, working as fast as reasonably possible.

Before starting to paint a door, wedge it open so there is room to walk through the doorway without touching wet paint, and also so that the hinged edge of the door can be reached easily. Remove handles, locks and other fittings; wedge a length of dowel in the latch hole to make a temporary handle for use until the paint has dried. Slide a dust sheet (drop cloth) underneath the door to catch any drips. Finally, warn everyone else in the house that the door is covered with wet paint, and keep children and pets out of the way in another room or out of doors.

PAINTING FLUSH DOORS

1 Remove the door furniture and wedge the door open. Then divide it up into eight or ten imaginary squares, and start painting at the top of the door by filling in the first square. Brush the paint out towards the door edges so it does not build up on the external angles.

2 Move on to the next block at the top of the door, brushing paint out towards the top and side edges as before. Carefully blend the two areas together with horizontal brushstrokes, then with light vertical laying-off strokes.

3 Continue to work down the door surface block by block, blending the wet edges of adjacent blocks together as they are painted. Always aim to complete a flush door in one session to prevent the joints between blocks showing up as hard lines. Replace the door furniture when the paint is touch-dry.

PAINTING PANELLED DOORS

1 Tackle panelled doors by painting the mouldings (**1**) around the recessed panels first. Take care not to let paint build up in the corners or to stray onto the faces of the cross-rails at this stage. Then paint the recessed panels (**2**).

2 Next, paint the horizontal cross-rails (**3**), brushing lightly inwards towards the painted panel mouldings to leave a sharp paint edge. Feather the paint out thinly where it runs onto the vertical stiles at each end of the rails.

3 Finish the door by painting the vertical centre rail (**4**) and the outer stiles (**5**), again brushing towards the panel mouldings. Where the rail abuts the cross-rails, finish with light brushstrokes parallel to the cross-rails.

PAINTING DOOR EDGES

Where the two faces of a door are being painted in two different colours, the convention is to match the colour of the hinged edge to that of the closing face of the door – the one facing the next room – and to paint the leading edge to match the other door face.

1 HINGED EDGE

VARNISHING WOOD

1 On bare wood, use a clean lint-free cloth to wipe the first coat onto the wood, working along the grain direction. This coat acts as a primer/sealer.

2 Sand the first coat lightly when dry to remove any 'nibs' caused by dust particles settling on the wet varnish, then wipe off the sanding dust.

3 Apply the second and subsequent coats of varnish with a brush, applying it along the grain and linking up adjacent areas with light brush strokes.

PAINTING WINDOWS

Windows are more difficult to paint than doors because they contain so many different surfaces, especially small-paned types criss-crossed with slim glazing bars (muntins). There is also the additional problem of paint straying onto the glass. The ideal is a neat paint line that covers the bedding putty and extends onto the glass surface by about 3 mm (⅛ in) to seal the joint and prevent condensation from running down between putty and glass.

With hinged windows, the edges of the casement or top opening light (transom) should be painted to match the colour used on the inside of the window. With double-hung sliding sash windows, the top and bottom edges of each sash and the top, bottom and sides of the frame are all painted to match the inner face of the sashes.

Remove the window hardware before you start painting. On casement windows tap a nail into the bottom edge of the casement and into the lower frame rebate and link them with stiff wire to stop the casement from swinging open or shut.

For best results, sash windows should be removed from their frames before painting. Modern spring-mounted windows are easy to release from their frames. With older cord-operated types, remove the staff beads (window stops) first to free the sashes. Although quite a major task, take the opportunity to renew the sash cords (pulley ropes). This makes it possible to cut the cords to free the window. Some making good and finishing off will have to be done after the window is reassembled.

PAINTING A CASEMENT WINDOW

1 Remove the window furniture from the opening casement and wedge the window open while you work. Tackle the glazing bars (muntins) and edge mouldings first (**1**), then the face of the surrounding casement frame (**2**) and finally the hinged edge of the casement. Paint the other edges from outside.

2 Move on to paint the glazing bars and edge mouldings (**3**) of the fixed casement. Use masking tape or a paint shield to ensure neat, straight edges here and on the opening casement; the paint should overlap the glass by about 3 mm (⅛ in). Paint the face of the surrounding casement frame (**4**).

PAINTING A SASH WINDOW

1 To paint sash windows without removing the sashes from their frames, start by raising the bottom (inner) sash and lowering the top (outer) one. Paint the lower half of the top sash (**1**), including its bottom edge, and the exposed parting beads at the top and bottom (**2**) and the exposed sides of the frame itself.

2 When the paint is touch-dry, reverse the sash positions and paint the upper half of the top sash (**3**), including its top edge, and the exposed and unpainted parting beads and frame sides (**4**).

PAINTING AROUND GLASS

3 Paint the outer frame (**5**), then the centre frame member between the opening and fixed casements (**6**). Complete the job by painting the window sill (**7**) and the rebate into which the opening casement closes.

1 Stick masking tape to the glass with its edge 3 mm (⅛ in) from the wood. Paint the surrounding wood, removing the tape when the paint is touch-dry.

2 Alternatively, hold a paint shield against the edge of the glazing bar (muntin) or surrounding moulding while painting. Wipe the shield regularly to prevent smears.

USING STAIN

TIP

To clean up an untidy paint edge on the glass, use a ruler and a very sharp knife to cut a clean edge, and carefully scrape off the excess paint up to the cut line.

3 Finish off by painting the face and edges of the inner sash (**5**), the staff beads and any other trim mouldings around the window (**6**). Finally, paint the window sill (**7**). Leave the sashes ajar until the paint has dried to avoid components sticking.

Test the stain on an offcut of the same wood, or in an inconspicuous area. If necessary, dilute it. Use a clean lint-free cloth to apply stain to bare wood. If the result is too pale, apply further coats when the first is dry. Avoid overlapping parallel bands of stain; the overlap will show up as a darker area when the stain dries.

PAPERHANGING

The term 'wall coverings' is used to describe the whole range of decorative materials sold in roll form and designed to be stuck to wall and ceiling surfaces with a strippable adhesive. The range includes an enormous variety of designs, patterns and colourways . . . almost too many, as any home decorator will testify when confronted by an array of pattern books and trying to decide which covering to select.

The vast majority of wall coverings are either made entirely from paper, or have a plastic or cloth layer bonded to a paper backing so that they can be hung in the same way as all-paper types. The basic technology of paperhanging has changed little over the centuries, even if the products have been subtly altered and improved; people still paper the living room in a way that would be familiar to their grandparents.

The two main developments that have occurred in recent years are the introduction of ready-pasted types which are immersed in a trough of water instead of having paste brushed onto them, and of all-plastic wall coverings which are hung by pasting the wall.

This chapter gives practical information on choosing the paperhanging tools, materials and other equipment needed to hang or strip wall coverings. There is advice on how to go about removing existing wall decorations – other wall coverings, materials such as texture paints, wall panelling and tiles of various types – and on preparing the surface. This is followed by detailed step-by-step instructions on how to hang a new wall covering on walls and ceilings; and on how to cope with awkward areas such as door and window openings, arches and stairwells.

OPPOSITE
There is virtually no limit to the versatility of modern wall coverings. This complementary match of broken colour and simple stripes is linked by a striking multicoloured border at dado (chair) rail level.

PAPERHANGING TOOLS AND EQUIPMENT

As for painting, there are two distinct groups of tools, equipment and materials to deal with wall coverings.

Stripping tools

The basic technique for removing an old wall covering is to soften the paste used to stick it to the wall so that it can be scraped off and discarded. To strip porous materials such as ordinary printed paper and the backing paper left behind after dry-stripping vinyl wall covering, use a bucket of water and a sponge or a garden spray gun to apply the water, dust sheets (drop cloths) to protect floor coverings, and a broad-bladed scraping knife to remove the softened paper.

To remove wall coverings with a water-resistant plastic or painted surface, it is necessary to pierce the surface film and so allow the water to penetrate. This can be done with a serrated wallpaper scraper or preferably a toothed roller or wheels, which is rolled backwards and forwards over the surface to create hundreds of little perforations. The water will take longer to penetrate this type of wall covering.

Stripping can be speeded up dramatically on coated wall coverings (and also on paper-backed fabrics and texture paints) by using a steam stripper. This consists of a perforated steaming plate and a water reservoir heated by electricity or bottled gas. Steam penetrates the surface far more quickly than water does, enabling the covering to be stripped quickly and effectively.

Paperhanging tools

There are four separate operations involved in hanging a new wall covering: cutting to length, pasting, hanging and trimming.

For cutting, the tools are a retractable steel tape measure, a pencil and a pair of scissors (or a sharp utility knife and a steel straightedge).

For pasting the wall covering, there should be a bucket in which to mix the paste (unless using ready-mixed tub paste), plus a stirrer and a brush with which to apply the paste. A 100 mm (4 in) wide paintbrush is satisfactory, but a special pasting brush can be bought.

As far as choosing the correct paste is concerned, follow the instructions for the wall covering concerned. In particular, remember that a paste containing a fungicide should be used for washable and vinyl coverings, to prevent mould from growing in the paste as it slowly dries under the impervious covering. A special overlap adhesive will be needed for lap joints in internal and external corners when using washables or vinyls.

When hanging a ready-pasted wall covering, the table, bucket and brush can be dispensed with. All that is needed is a plastic soaking trough in which to immerse the rolled-up lengths of wall covering.

Before starting hanging, a plumb bob and line are needed to mark a true vertical line on the wall against which to hang the first length.

Most wall coverings are applied with a special soft-bristled paperhanging brush. These are generally between 190 and 250 mm (7½ to 10 in) wide, and have a slim handle. The soft bristles help to make the wall covering follow the contours of the wall surface behind, and also eliminate undue hand contact with the face of the covering, which might mark it.

A sponge can be used instead of a brush for hanging washables or vinyls, especially if they are ready-pasted, since here the sponge helps mop water from the surface of the wall covering as well as smoothing it into place.

The final stage is trimming, and the best tool for this is a special pair of paperhangers' scissors. These have blades up to 300 mm (12 in) long for making long, straight cuts.

For papering walls a stepladder is needed which should be tall enough to enable the ceiling to be easily touched. For papering ceilings, set up a proper platform across the width of the room at a comfortable height, using scaffold boards or staging on trestles or other low supports to ensure complete stability. Do not step from chair to chair or set up similar makeshift arrangements.

PASTING TABLES

A flat surface is needed to lay the paper on while it is being pasted. It is best to use a proper pasting table. This is a lightweight folding table covered in hardboard or plywood on a softwood frame, and is usually about 1.8 m (6 ft) long and just wider than a standard roll of wall covering. If you cannot buy, borrow or hire a pasting table, one can be improvised by cutting a standard sheet of plywood or chipboard (particle board) down to the same width and supporting it on trestles or sawhorses.

SEAM ROLLERS

For smooth wall coverings, a tool called a seam roller can be used to make sure that the seams are well bonded to the wall. Do not use a seam roller on textured or embossed wall coverings, though, as it will flatten the embossing.

Displayed on a fold-up pasting table are a soaking trough (1), rubber gloves (2), sponge (3), pencil (4), sharp utility knife (5), paperhangers' scissors (6), plumb bob and line (7), retractable steel tape measure (8), steel straightedge (9), paste bucket (10), pasting brush (11), packet of ready-mixed paste (12), seam roller (13) and paperhanging brush (14). A spirit level (15) can do double duty in checking verticals and as a straightedge.

PREPARING FOR PAPERHANGING

Unrestricted access is a must for paperhanging. If working on just the walls, move all the furniture to the centre of the room and cover it with dust sheets (drop cloths). When tackling the ceiling too, it is best to remove all the furniture completely if there is space to store it elsewhere in the house; otherwise group it at one end of the room so that most of the ceiling can be done, and then move it to the other end to complete the job.

Next, take down curtains and blinds (drapes and shades) and remove wall-mounted or ceiling-mounted tracks. Turn off the electricity supply at the mains, then disconnect and remove wall or ceiling light fittings as necessary, covering the bare wire ends thoroughly with insulating tape before restoring the power supply to the rest of the house. In the USA, ceiling roses, wall switch plates and socket outlets can be unscrewed and removed without disconnecting the wall receptacles or switches. Isolate, drain, disconnect and remove radiators, and unscrew their wall brackets. Call in a professional electrician or plumber for these jobs if unsure of how to do them safely.

Lift down pictures, and remove other wall-mounted fittings such as shelves and display units. To make it easy to relocate the screw holes afterwards, push a matchstick (wooden match) into each one (see Tip).

CHOOSING THE STARTING POINT

ABOVE Start paperhanging at the centre of a chimney breast (fireplace projection) if the wall covering has a large, dominant pattern. Otherwise start next to the door so the inevitable pattern break can be disguised above it.

RIGHT Work outwards from the centre of a dormer window so the design is centred on the window recess.

ESTIMATING WALL COVERINGS (WALLS)

Height	Distance around room																	
	9m 30ft	10m 33ft	12m 40ft	13m 42ft	14m 46ft	15m 50ft	16m 52ft	17m 56ft	19m 62ft	20m 66ft	21m 69ft	22m 72ft	23m 75ft	25m 82ft	26m 85ft	27m 88ft	28m 92ft	30m 98ft
2.15–2.30 m / 7–7½ ft	4	5	5	6	6	7	7	8	8	9	9	10	10	11	12	12	13	13
2.30–2.45 m / 7½–8 ft	5	5	6	6	7	7	8	8	9	9	10	10	11	11	12	13	13	14
2.45–2.60 m / 8–8½ ft	5	5	6	7	7	8	9	9	10	10	11	12	12	13	14	14	15	15
2.60–2.75 m / 8½–9 ft	5	5	6	7	7	8	9	9	10	10	11	12	12	13	14	14	15	15
2.75–2.90 m / 9–9½ ft	6	6	7	7	8	9	9	10	10	11	12	12	13	14	14	15	15	16
2.90–3.05 m / 9½–10 ft	6	6	7	8	8	9	10	10	11	12	12	13	14	14	15	16	16	17
3.05–3.20 m / 10–10½ ft	6	7	8	8	9	10	10	11	12	13	13	14	15	16	16	17	18	19

Numbers are based on a standard roll size of 10.05 m (33 ft) long and 520 mm (20½ in) wide. The measurement around the room includes all windows and doorway.

If the walls and ceiling are at present painted, they need washing down to remove dirt, grease, smoke stains and the like. If they are decorated with another wall covering, this will have to be removed and any defects in the surface put right. Finally, they need sizing – treating with a diluted coat of wallpaper adhesive to even out the porosity of the surface and to help to improve the 'slip' of the pasted wall covering during hanging.

Measuring up
The next job is to estimate how many rolls of wall covering will be needed to decorate the room. If using a material that comes in standard-sized rolls, simply measure the room dimensions and refer to the charts given here for the number of rolls needed to cover the walls and ceiling. They allow for a typical door and window area; fewer rolls are needed for a room with large picture windows or wide door openings. If using a paper-backed cloth covering which comes in a nonstandard width, measure up each wall, and ask the supplier to estimate what length of material you will need; such materials

are too expensive to waste. Wall coverings in the USA vary in width and length but are usually available in rolls sized to cover a specified area, allowing for trimming.

Buying wall coverings
Wall coverings are made in batches, with a number printed on the label, and it is important to check that there are

sufficient rolls with the same batch number; colours may not match exactly between batches.

When hanging a wall covering with a particularly large pattern repeat, wastage is often unusually high and it may be wise to purchase one or two extra rolls, over and above the numbers given in the charts. Most suppliers will take back unopened rolls.

ESTIMATING WALL COVERINGS (CEILINGS)

Distance around room		No of
m	ft	rolls
10	33	2
11	36	2
12	40	2
13	42	3
14	46	3
15	50	4
16	52	4
17	56	4
18	59	5
19	62	5
20	66	5
21	69	6
22	72	7
23	75	7

TIP

Insert a matchstick (wooden match) in each hole left when unscrewing wall-mounted fixtures and fittings that will be replaced later. It will burst through the wall covering as this is applied and make it easy to find the screw holes.

STRIPPING OLD WALL COVERINGS

In the days when ordinary printed wall coverings were all that were usually on sale, it was common practice to paper over existing wallpaper, often to the point where four or five successive layers would accumulate. This is no longer considered acceptable (and will not work at all over today's washable and vinyl wall coverings), and it is always best to strip all old coverings before hanging new ones. Even if the old material looks sound, hanging a newly-pasted wall covering over it may cause it to lift from the wall, creating ugly bubbles that are impossible to disguise. This also applies to the backing paper that is left on the wall after dry-stripping a vinyl wall covering; there is no guarantee that it is perfectly bonded to the wall, and so hanging another wall covering over it could give very poor results.

Once the room is cleared and dust sheets (drop cloths) are spread over the floor and any remaining furniture, the next step is to identify what type of wall covering is to be removed. An ordinary printed paper will absorb water splashed on it immediately; other types will not. To tell washables from vinyls, pick and lift a corner and try to strip the wall covering dry. The printed plastic layer of a vinyl wall covering will peel off dry, but the surface of a washable paper will not come off in the same way unless it is a duplex paper made in two layers. With paper-backed fabric wall coverings, it is often possible to peel the fabric away from its paper backing; try it before turning to other more complicated methods of removal.

1 To strip printed wallpapers, wet the surface with a sponge or a garden spray gun. Wait for the water to penetrate, and repeat if necessary.

2 Using a stiff wallpaper scraper – not a filling knife (putty knife) – start scraping the old paper from the wall at a seam. Wet it again while working if necessary.

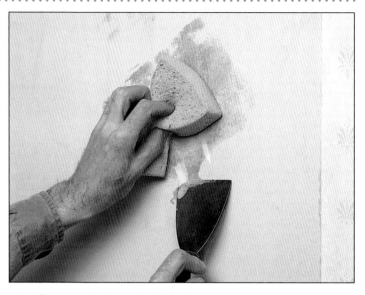

3 Turn off the power before stripping around switches and other fittings, then loosen the faceplate screws to strip the wallpaper behind them.

4 After removing the bulk of the old wallpaper, go back over the wall surface and remove any remaining 'nibs' of paper with sponge/spray gun and scraper.

5 To strip a washable wallpaper, start by scoring the plastic coating with a serrated scraper or toothed roller, then soak and scrape as before.

6 For quicker results, use a steam stripper to remove washable papers. Press the steaming plate to the next area while stripping the area just steamed.

STRIPPING VINYLS

1 Strip vinyl wall coverings by lifting a corner to separate the vinyl layer from the paper backing. Strip it off by pulling it away from the wall surface.

2 Always soak and remove the plain backing paper left on the wall after stripping a vinyl. It may well not be a sound lining for a new wall covering.

REMOVING OTHER OLD FINISHES

If the wall or ceiling to be given a new covering is painted or wallpapered, preparing the surface for its new finish is quite straightforward. However, if it was previously covered with materials such as texture paint, ceramic or polystyrene tiles or wall panelling, more work will be needed to remove the old finishes and return the surface to its original condition.

Textured finishes are tackled in different ways, depending on their type. Texture paints are basically thick water-based (latex) paints, normally used to create relatively low-relief effects, and can be removed with specially formulated paint removers. Some textured effects formed with a powder or ready-mixed compound are best removed with a steam wallpaper stripper, which softens the compound so that it can be scraped from the wall.

Never attempt to sand off a textured finish. There are two reasons. The first is that it will create huge quantities of very fine dust; the second is that older versions of this product contained asbestos fibres as a filler, and any action that might release these into the atmosphere as inhalable dust must be avoided at all costs.

For tiles and wall panelling, complete removal or a cover-up with plasterboard (gypsum board) are the two options available. The former will leave a surface in need of considerable renovation, while the latter will cause a slight loss of space within the room, as well as some complications at door and window openings.

REMOVING TEXTURED FINISHES

1 Strip texture paint by brushing on a generous coat of a proprietary texture paint remover. Stipple it well into the paint and leave it to penetrate.

2 When the paint has softened, scrape it off with a broad-bladed scraper. Wear gloves, and also safety goggles if working on a ceiling.

3 Once the bulk of the coating is removed, use wire wool dipped in the paint remover to strip off any remaining flecks of paint.

4 Remove powder-based or ready-mixed types using a steam stripper, which will soften the finish. Never try to sand off this type of finish.

REMOVING CERAMIC TILES

1 On a completely tiled wall, use a hammer to crack a tile and create a starting point for the stripping. On partly tiled walls, start at the tile edge.

2 Use a broad bolster (stonecutter's) chisel and a club (spalling) hammer to chip the old tiles off the wall. Have the wall replastered afterwards rather than trying to patch the surface up.

REMOVING POLYSTYRENE TILES

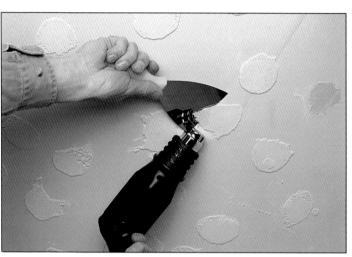

1 Lever the tiles away from the ceiling with a scraper. If they were fixed with a continuous coat of adhesive, consider covering the tiles with heavy lining paper as a temporary measure. For the best finish, fit a new plasterboard (gypsum board) ceiling, nailing through the tile layer into the ceiling joists.

2 If the tiles were fixed in place with blobs of adhesive, use a heat gun to soften the old adhesive so it can be removed with a broad-bladed scraper.

REMOVING WALL PANELLING

1 The last board to be fixed will have been nailed to the fixing grounds through its face. Use a nail punch to drive the nails in and free the board.

2 The other boards will have been secret-nailed through their tongues. Use a crowbar (wrecking bar) to prise them away from their grounds.

3 Finally, prise the grounds off the wall, and use a claw hammer or crowbar with some protective packing to lever the fixing nails out of the wall.

PREPARING SURFACES FOR COVERING

Once the previous wall and ceiling decorations have been removed the next task is to restore any defects in the surfaces to be covered, and then to prepare them so that they present the perfect substrate for successful paperhanging.

The first step is to put down some heavy-duty plastic sheeting on the floor to catch splashes, and then to wash down the bare wall and ceiling surfaces thoroughly with strong household detergent or sugar soap (all-purpose cleaner), working from the bottom up on walls, and then to rinse them off with clean water, working this time from top to bottom on walls. Turn off the electricity supply first in case water gets into light switches and socket outlets (receptacles). Leave the surfaces to dry out thoroughly.

Next, repair defects such as cracks, holes and other surface damage which may have been concealed by the previous decorations, or even caused by their removal.

Finally, treat the wall and ceiling surfaces with a coat of size or diluted wallpaper paste, and leave this to dry before starting paperhanging. Size seals porous plaster, providing a surface with even absorption, and also makes it easier to slide the pasted lengths of wall covering into position on the wall.

PREPARING WALLS AND CEILINGS

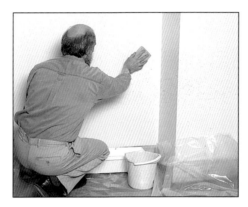

1 Wash wall surfaces down with sugar soap (all-purpose cleaner) or detergent, working from the bottom up, then rinse them with clean water, working from the top down.

2 Wash ceilings with a floor mop or squeegee, after disconnecting and removing light fittings. Again, rinse off with clean water.

3 Fill cracks, holes and other defects in the wall and ceiling surfaces as appropriate, leave the filler to harden and then sand the repair down flush.

4 Apply a coat of size or diluted wallpaper paste to wall and ceiling surfaces that are to be papered, and leave them to dry before starting paperhanging.

CROSS-LINING

If the wall surface is in poor condition, has been previously decorated with gloss paint or is being decorated with a thin fabric wall covering, it is best to hang lining (liner) paper first. This is usually hung horizontally rather than vertically, with butt joints between lengths and with ends and edges trimmed just short of adjacent ceiling and wall surfaces. Use the same type of paste for the lining paper as for the subsequent wall covering.

MEASURING AND CUTTING TO LENGTH

1 For quick and easy calculations, mark the whole length of the pasting table at 300 mm (12 in) intervals with a pencil and metal straightedge.

2 Measure the length of wall covering needed for the drop, including trim allowances, and mark this on the paper. Cut the first piece to length.

PASTING WALL COVERINGS

1 Face the light to make it easy to spot any unpasted areas – they look dull, not shiny. Apply a generous band of paste down the centre of the length.

2 Align one edge of the wall covering with the edge of the pasting table, then brush the paste out towards that edge from the centre band.

3 Draw the length across to the other edge of the table, and apply paste out to that edge too. Check that there are no dry or thinly pasted areas.

4 Continue pasting until the end of the table is reached. Then lift the pasted end of the wall covering and fold it over on itself, pasted side to pasted side.

5 Slide the paper along the table so the folded section hangs down. Paste the rest of the length and fold the other end over on itself as before.

HANGING THE FIRST LENGTHS

The first length of wall covering must be hung correctly if the decoration of the rest of the room is to go according to plan. Therefore the first thing to do is to decide on exactly where this is to be hung. The usual starting point is close to the door, just less than the wall covering's width away from the frame, so that the inevitable pattern discontinuity that will occur on returning to the starting point can be concealed on the short join above the door. If using a wall covering with a large design motif in a room which has a chimney breast (fireplace projection) it is preferable to start paperhanging on the chimney breast itself so that the design can be centred on it. When papering only part of a room, the starting point should be just less than the width of the wall covering from one corner of the room, to allow the edge of the covering to be trimmed accurately into the corner angle.

Next, use a roll of wall covering as a yardstick and mark off successive widths round the room walls with a pencil to check that there will not be any joins on external corners such as the sides of window reveals. If these occur, move the starting point along by about 50 mm (2 in) and recheck the join positions all round.

Finally, mark a true vertical line on the wall at the chosen starting point, using a pencil and a plumb bob and line. Failure to do this could result in the pattern running seriously out of true as successive lengths are hung.

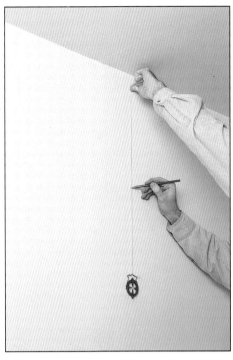

1 At the chosen starting point, use a plumb bob and line to mark a vertical line on the wall surface. Join up the pencil marks with a straightedge.

2 Fetch the first length of pasted wall covering after leaving it to soak for the time recommended on the label. Carry it draped over the arm.

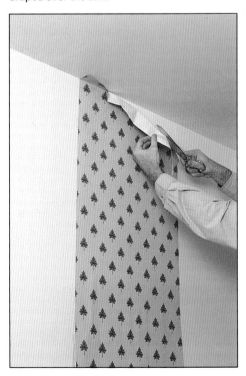

6 Peel the end of the length away from the wall so the excess can be trimmed with scissors. Brush the end back into place. Repeat at the bottom.

3 Unfold the upper flap and press the top edge of the length against the wall. Slide it across the wall until the edge lines up with the marked line.

4 Use a paperhanging brush (or a sponge for washables and vinyls) to smooth the wall covering into place. Work from the middle out towards the edges.

5 Use a pencil or the curved back of paperhanging scissors blades to mark the trimming line at ceiling level. Do the same at floor level.

7 Hang the next drop with the lengths exactly edge to edge. Brush the wall covering into the wall/ceiling angle and into the internal angle.

8 On flat wall coverings, run a seam roller down the join to ensure that it sticks securely. Never use a seam roller on embossed or relief wall coverings.

TIP

If a seam refuses to lie flat because it was inadequately pasted and has begun to dry out, brush a little extra paste underneath it and roll it again.

PAPERHANGING AROUND CORNERS

In a perfect world, rooms would have corners that were truly square and truly vertical, and it would be possible to hang wall covering all around the room in a continuous operation, simply turning the lengths that ran into the room corners straight onto the adjoining walls. In reality, corners are seldom square or true, and if the covering was hung in this way, lengths would be vertical on the first wall but could be running well off the vertical by the time they returned to the starting point. The effect can be visually disastrous, with vertical pattern elements clearly out of alignment at corners and horizontal pattern features sloping relative to the ceiling or skirting (baseboard).

The way to avoid these problems is to complete each wall with a cut-down strip that only just turns onto the next wall, to conceal the join in the corner angle. Then hang the remainder of the strip with its machine-cut edge against a newly drawn vertical line on the second wall, so that its other edge can be trimmed to follow the internal angle precisely. Any slight pattern discontinuity that results will not be noticeable except to the closest scrutiny, and the remaining lengths on the second wall will be hung truly vertically. A similar process is used when paperhanging around external corners, as at window reveals and on chimney breasts (fireplace projections).

PAPERING INTERNAL CORNERS

1 Hang the last full length before the corner of the room, then measure the distance to the corner from the edge of the length and add about 12 mm (½ in).

2 Use a pencil and straightedge to mark a strip of the required width, measured from the relevant edge (here, the left one), and cut it from the length.

3 Paste the strip and hang it in the usual way, allowing the hand-cut edge to lap onto the adjoining wall. Trim the top and bottom edges as usual.

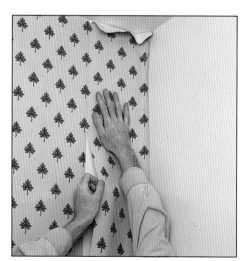

4 Brush the tongue into the internal angle. If it will not lie flat because the corner is out of true, make small release cuts in the edge and brush it flat.

5 Measure the width of the remaining strip, subtract 12 mm (½ in) and mark a fresh vertical line on the adjoining wall at this distance from the corner.

6 Hang the strip to the marked line, brushing the wall covering into the angle so it just turns onto the surface of the first wall.

7 Use the back of the scissors blades to mark the line of the corner on the wall covering, then cut along the line and smooth the cut edge back into the angle. Use special overlap adhesive when using washables and vinyls on all lap joints.

PAPERING EXTERNAL CORNERS

1 Plan the starting point so that lengths turn external corners by about 25 mm (1 in). Brush the paper onto the next wall, making small cuts so it lies flat.

2 Carefully tear off a narrow strip of the wall covering along the turned edge to leave a 'feathered' edge that will not show through the next length.

3 Mark a vertical line on the next wall surface at a distance from the corner equal to the width of the wall covering plus about 6 mm (¼ in).

4 Hang the next full length to the marked line, with its other edge overlapping the feathered edge of the strip turned from the previous wall.

5 Brush this length into position, trim it at top and bottom as before, and run a seam roller down the overlap (not on embossed or textured wall coverings). Again, use a special overlap adhesive with washables and vinyls.

PAPERHANGING AROUND DOORS AND WINDOWS

Paperhanging on flat, uninterrupted walls is quite straightforward, calling only for the basic positioning and trimming techniques. Turning corners is only slightly more difficult. The trouble is that rooms also contain doors, windows and wall-mounted fittings and fixtures such as light switches and socket outlets (receptacles). Paperhanging around these obstacles can be tricky, but there are procedures for dealing with them.

Doors and window frames fitted flush with the internal wall surface present few problems; all that is necessary is to trim the wall covering so it finishes flush with the edge of the architrave (trim) or casing. Where the window or door is recessed, some careful patching-in of extra pieces is needed to cover all the surfaces of the reveal. It is also important to select the starting point to avoid joins between lengths falling on the external corners of such reveals; always check this point before beginning paperhanging, and adjust the starting point by about 50 mm (2 in) if it will occur.

Paperhanging round electrical fittings (fixtures) is not so difficult. The idea is to make diagonal cuts over the faceplate, cut away most of the resulting triangular tongues and tuck what is left behind the loosened faceplate. Always turn the power supply to the accessory off first. Do not do this with vinyl foils, which can conduct electricity; instead, simply trim the covering flush with the edges of the accessory faceplate. In the USA wall plates and socket outlets can be removed separately without disconnecting the wall receptacles or switches, which makes the task much simpler.

PAPERING AROUND FLUSH DOORS AND WINDOWS

1 On reaching a flush door or window frame, hang the previous length as normal. Then hang the next length to overlap the door or window frame.

2 Cut away the unwanted wall covering to within about 25 mm (1 in) of the edge of the architrave (trim) or window casing, and discard the waste strip.

3 Press the covering against the frame so that its corner is visible, and make a diagonal cut from the waste edge of the paper to the mark.

4 Use the paperhanging brush to press the tongues of paper well into the angles between the wall and the door architrave or window casing.

5 Peel back the tongues carefully and cut along the marked lines with paperhanging scissors. Then brush the trimmed edges back into position.

PAPERING AROUND RECESSED DOORS AND WINDOWS

1 On reaching a recessed door or window frame, hang the previous length as normal. Then hang the next length, allowing it to overlap the recess.

2 Make a horizontal cut into the overlapping edge level with the underside of the reveal to allow the central portion of the length to cover the side wall.

PAPERING AROUND ELECTRICAL FITTINGS (FIXTURES)

3 On recessed windows, make a similar cut lower down the length, level with the top surface of the window sill. Then trim it to fit round the end of the sill.

4 Cut a patch to fit on the underside of the reveal, big enough to turn onto adjoining wall and frame surfaces. Press it well into the internal angles.

Make diagonal cuts towards the corners, trim off the triangles and tuck the edges behind the loosened faceplate. The power must be turned off first.

5 Tear along the edges of the patch that will be covered when the piece above the reveal and the tongue covering its side wall are brushed into place.

6 Trim the edges of the patch and tongue to meet the frame neatly. Then hang full widths when the other side of the reveal is reached, and repeat steps 1–6.

PAPERING STAIRWELLS

Paperhanging in stairwells is no different in principle from work in any other room. However, the job is made more difficult by the need to handle longer lengths of wall covering, and also because access to the higher reaches of the stairwell walls can be awkward. It is a job that requires careful planning, and is best tackled with the assistance of a second person.

First of all, work out the starting point. It is best to hang the longest drop – the one that reaches from landing ceiling to hall floor – first of all. Mark its position and check that other joins will not fall awkwardly round the rest of the stairwell, especially if it has a window opening onto it. Adjust the starting point if necessary.

The next thing to do is to work out how to gain access to the various wall surfaces involved without obstructing passage up and down the stairwell or blocking off the walls themselves. On a straight flight it may be possible to use components from a hired slot-together scaffold tower to make a suitable working platform. On flights with quarter or half-landings it will probably be necessary to tailor-make an assembly of ladder sections, stepladders, homemade supports and scaffold boards; two typical arrangements are shown in the illustrations. Nail scrap wood to stair treads to locate ladder feet securely, and lock scaffold boards together by drilling holes through them where they overlap and dropping a bolt through the holes (no need for a nut). Note that ladders or steps shown resting against wall surfaces will have to be repositioned as the work progresses.

ACCESS EQUIPMENT FOR STAIRWELLS

Use a selection of ladders, steps, scaffold boards and homemade supports to construct a platform that allows access to all the wall surfaces being decorated without obstructing the stairs themselves.

STARTING POINT

Aim to start work by hanging the longest drop first. Then work along the stairwell walls in sequence, turning corners and tackling obstacles as for other rooms.

1 Fold up long lengths of wall covering concertina-fashion with the top end of the length uppermost, and carry them to the stairs supported over the arm.

2 Get a helper to support the folds of wall covering while positioning the top end of the length on the stairwell wall against a vertical line.

3 When measuring lengths that will meet a dado (chair) rail or skirting (baseboard) at an angle, remember to measure the longer edge of the length.

4 Where the bottom edge of the length meets a shaped skirting, make small release cuts in the edge and trim it to follow the curve.

PAPERING AROUND OBSTACLES

Where the end of a handrail fits flush with the wall, cut the lower part of the length into two strips so their edges can be trimmed around the rail and joined edge to edge beneath it. Use a similar technique to fit the wall covering around a flush newel post.

PAPERING CEILINGS

Many people regard the papering of ceilings with horror. In reality they are easier to deal with than walls because they are flat, do not have any awkward angles (except in rooms with sloping ceilings and dormer windows), and have few obstacles attached to them apart from the occasional light fitting (fixture), which can in any case usually be removed quite easily.

The only thing that takes getting used to when papering ceilings is working on an upside-down surface, but the basic technique is no different from working on walls. The wall covering is simply positioned, brushed into place and then trimmed where it meets adjoining surfaces.

The most important thing to plan carefully is access equipment that will allow a complete length to be hung across the room. Nothing is more dangerous than attempting to step from chair to chair; proper access is a must. The best solution is to use scaffold boards or lengths of staging, supported by stepladders, trestles or homemade supports to create a flat, level walkway spanning the room from wall to wall at a height that allows the ceiling to be reached comfortably. It will take only a few seconds to reposition after hanging each length, ready for the next.

This is also a job where an additional pair of hands will be a big help, at least before gaining the knack of supporting a concertina of pasted wall covering with one hand while brushing it into position with the other. This can be done only with practice.

The first length should be hung to a guideline on the ceiling. The best way of marking this is with a chalked line, held against the ceiling at both ends and snapped against it. Use red chalk for a white ceiling.

1 Paste the wall covering in the usual way, but fold it up concertina-fashion with the starting end of the length folded over on itself. Lining (liner) paper has been used here.

ACCESS EQUIPMENT FOR CEILINGS

Set up an access platform across the room, using scaffold boards supported on staging or stepladders, to create a walkway at a height that allows the ceiling to be comfortably reached.

2 Hang the first length to a chalked line just less than the width of the wall covering from the side wall. Support the folds on a spare roll of wall covering.

PAPERING ARCHES

The shape of an arch makes it impossible to get a pattern match along the curved join. It is best to choose a wall covering with a small design motif and a random pattern, to use different but complementary designs for the face walls and the arch surface, or to use lining (liner) paper inside the arch and paint it a plain colour.

To paper an arched recess, cover the face and back walls first, turning cut tongues of wall covering onto the arched surface. Then cover the arch surface as described below.

3 Trim the overlaps at the ends and along the side wall. Then hang the second length in the same way, butted up against the edge of the first length.

4 On meeting a pendant light fitting (fixture) pierce the wall covering over its centre and make a series of radial cuts outwards from the pierced point.

5 With the power turned off at the mains, unscrew the cover and trim the tongues off flush with the base of the fitting. Replace the cover to conceal the cut ends.

6 Where the ceiling runs into an alcove, cut the wall covering in line with the side wall of the recess and brush it into place. Trim off the waste section.

To paper a through archway, hang the wall covering on the two face walls and trim out the waste to leave an overlap of about 25 mm (1 in) all around. Make cuts in the edge so that the tongues can be turned onto the arch surface. Then cut a strip of wall covering a fraction narrower than the width of the arch surface and long enough to cover it in one piece, and brush this into place. Work from the bottom of one side upwards to the top of the arch, and then down the other side. Always use special overlap adhesive with washables and vinyls.

OTHER PAPERHANGING TECHNIQUES

Apart from the traditional method of pasting the wall covering on a pasting table and then hanging it on the wall, two other techniques may sometimes be needed. The first is hanging ready-pasted wall coverings, which are growing in popularity, while the second is hanging speciality wall coverings.

Hanging ready-pasted wall coverings could not be easier. The back of the wall covering – usually a washable or vinyl type, for obvious reasons – is coated during manufacture with an even layer of dried paste. To activate this, simply cut the length that is needed, roll it up with the top of the length on the outside of the roll, and immerse it in water. Special soaking troughs are sold by most wall covering suppliers, and are intended to be placed next to the skirting (baseboard) beneath the point where the length is to be hung. The trough is filled with cold (not hot) water, the length is immersed and drawn upwards onto the wall so that excess water drains back into the trough. It is then hung and trimmed in the usual way.

Many speciality wall coverings are designed to be hung by pasting the wall, not the wall covering. Some also have untrimmed edges, which need to be cut after overlapping adjoining lengths. The technique is, however, quite straightforward.

HANGING READY-PASTED WALL COVERINGS

1 Place the trough next to the wall, fill it with cold water and immerse the rolled-up length in it, top end outermost, for the recommended time.

2 At the end of the recommended soaking time, grasp the top end of the length and draw it upwards so that the excess water runs off it back into the trough.

3 Slide the top of the length into position on the wall, aligning it with a marked line or butting it up against its neighbour. Do not step in the trough.

4 Use a sponge rather than a paperhanging brush to smooth the length into place on the wall. This helps to absorb excess water from the surface.

1 Cut the wall covering to the length required, including a trim allowance, and roll it up face inwards around a broom handle or similar object.

2 Apply the recommended paste (usually a thick ready-mixed type) to the wall, and then unroll the wall covering onto the wet paste against a marked line.

3 Run a clean, dry paint roller backwards and forwards over the surface of the wall covering to bond it firmly to the wall.

4 Use a sharp utility knife – and a straightedge if needed – to trim the wall covering where it meets the ceiling and the skirting (baseboard).

5 To create neat joins, overlap adjoining lengths slightly and then cut through both layers with a sharp utility knife run along a straightedge.

6 Peel away the two waste strips and smooth the cut edges neatly back into place. Run a seam roller along the seam to ensure a good bond.

TILING

Tiles have a long pedigree in the interior decoration business. Faience (glazed earthenware) plaques have been found in Cretan buildings dating from around 1800 BC, and a tradition of ceramic wall and floor decoration was established soon after this farther east in Syria and Persia (now Iran). Mosaic wall and floor decorations, incorporating stone (usually marble), glass and ceramic tesserae, were also a major feature of Roman interiors. The technique spread to North Africa and thence to Spain, and the Renaissance soon led to widespread use of decorative tiling all over Europe.

Probably the most important centre of ceramic tile making in Europe was Holland, where the creation of individually handpainted tiles in a unique blue-grey colour soon made Delft famous in the early seventeenth century. From there, the use of tiles spread rapidly, and it was not long before mass production was introduced. The end product is the familiar ceramic tile we use today. The manufacturing and printing technology may have changed, and the adhesives and grouts used may have improved, but the result would be familiar to a seventeenth-century Dutchman.

The twentieth century has brought new kinds of tile, notably vinyl, lino and cork tiles which owe their existence to advances in plastics and resins technology. They offer a combination of properties that make them useful alternatives to ceramics in a wide range of situations, and are generally much less expensive.

This chapter concentrates on working with ceramic wall tiles, since they are the most popular of the types available. A wide range of situations is dealt with, from splashbacks to whole walls, including information on setting out tiling schemes, and working around obstacles such as door and window openings. There are also comprehensive sections on using other types of wall tiles, and on tiling floors.

OPPOSITE
Wall tiles have never been available in such a
profusion of styles and designs, ranging from
highly glazed plain types to more rustic versions
with matt or textured surfaces and patterns
that look as though they have been
handpainted.

TILING TOOLS AND EQUIPMENT

Tools for ceramic tiles

For almost any ceramic tiling job, large or small, the following are needed: tile adhesive; a notched adhesive spreader; some tile spacers; lengths of tile edge trim (optional); grout plus a flexible spreader; a steel tape measure; some lengths of 38 × 12 mm (1½ × ½ in) softwood battening (furring strips), plus masonry pins and a hammer for supporting the tiles on large wall areas; a spirit level; a tile cutter; a tile saw; a tile file; a piece of dowel for shaping the grout lines; a pencil and felt-tip pen; some sponges and cloths for wiping and polishing. Some silicone sealant or mastic (caulking) may also be needed for waterproofing joints where tiling abuts baths, basins and shower trays.

Tile cutters range from the basic – an angled cutting tip attached to a handle – to elaborate cutting jigs that guarantee perfectly accurate cuts every time. A tile saw is useful for making shaped cutouts to fit around obstacles such as pipework, and a tile file helps to smooth cut edges.

Both adhesive and grout for wall tiling are now usually sold ready-mixed in plastic tubs complete with a notched plastic spreader. For areas that will get the occasional splash or may suffer from condensation, a water-resistant adhesive and grout is perfectly adequate, but for surfaces such as shower cubicles which will have to withstand prolonged wetting it is essential to use both waterproof adhesive and waterproof grout. Always use waterproof grout on tiled worktops; ordinary grout will harbour germs.

Grout is generally white, but coloured grout is on sale and will make a feature of the grout lines (an effect that looks best with plain or fairly neutral patterned tiles).

TILING TOOLS, MATERIALS AND EQUIPMENT

These include a tile saw (**1**), adhesive (**2**), a polishing cloth (**3**), a spirit level (**4**), tile edge nippers (**5**), a tile cutter/snapper (**6**) or a tiling jig (**7**), a tile scriber (**8**), a tile cutter with width and angle jig (**9**), a heavy duty tile cutter (**10**), tile files (**11**) or a tile edge sander with abrasive strips (**12**), masking tape (**13**), masonry nails (**14**), a hammer (**15**), a homemade tile gauge (**16**), a retractable steel measure (**17**), a pencil (**18**), adhesive spreaders (**19** and **27**), a grout finisher (**20**) or dowel (**21**), tile edging trim (**22**), small and large tile spacers (**23**), a grout remover (**24**), a grout spreader (**25**), grout (**26**) and battens (furring strips) (**28**).

Ceramic floor tile adhesive is widely available in powder form as well as ready-mixed. It is best always to use a waterproof type (plus waterproof grout), even in theoretically dry areas.

Adhesive and grout are both sold in a range of sizes, sometimes labelled by weight, sometimes by volume; always check the coverage specified by the manufacturer on the packaging when buying, so as not to overbuy or run out halfway through the job.

Tools for cork, vinyl and lino tiles

Only a few simple tools are needed to lay cork and vinyl tiles, but, except for the self-adhesive type, special tile adhesive is required. This is sold ready-mixed in tubs, and usually comes complete with a notched spreader.

Special water-based adhesive is the type to choose for both cork and lino tiles; solvent-based contact adhesives were formerly the first choice, but their fumes are extremely unpleasant and also dangerously inflammable, and they are no longer recommended. For vinyl-coated cork tiles a special vinyl acrylic adhesive is needed. For vinyl tiles, an emulsion-type latex flooring adhesive is the best choice.

For unsealed cork tiles a sealer is required. Ordinary polyurethane varnish, as used for furniture, will do; there are also special floor sealers. Three coats will be needed.

Tools are simply a tape measure, a sharp utility knife and a steel straightedge for marking and cutting border tiles. A proprietary profile gauge with sliding steel or plastic needles makes it easy to cut tiles to fit round awkward obstacles such as architraves (trims) and pipework. But it is just as effective, and less costly, to cut a template from card or paper.

SETTING OUT TILED AREAS

The best way to practise tiling skills is to begin by covering just a small area such as a washbasin splashback, where setting out the tiles so that they are centred on the area concerned is a simple job and there is very little tile cutting to do.

For a larger area – a whole wall, or perhaps even a complete room – exactly the same techniques are used. The big difference is the sheer scale of the job, which makes the preliminary setting-out by far the most important part. The problem is that walls are seldom blank surfaces, and there may be a number of obstacles to tile around. Care must be taken to get the best fit around them with these inflexible tile squares, without needing to cut impossibly thin slivers to fill in gaps.

The most important thing to do is to plan precisely where the whole tiles will fall. On a flat, uninterrupted wall this is quite easy; simply find the centre line of the wall and plan the tiling to start from

there. However, there will probably be obstacles such as window reveals, door openings and built-in furniture in the room, all competing to be the centre of attention, and it will be necessary to work out the best 'centre point' while all the time trying to avoid having very thin cut tile borders and edges.

It is best to use a device called a *tiling gauge* – a batten (furring strip) marked out in tile widths – to work this out. The gauge is easy to make from a straight piece of timber about 1.2 m (4 ft) long, marked off with pencil lines to match the size of the tile. Use this to ensure that the tiles will be centred accurately on major features such as window reveals, with a border of cut tiles of equal width at the end of each row or column of tiles.

The next stage is the actual setting-out. With large areas of tiling, two things are vitally important. First, the tile rows must be exactly horizontal; if they are not, errors will accumulate as

the tiles extend across the wall, throwing the verticals out of alignment with disastrous results. When tiling right around a room, inaccurate levels mean that rows do not match up at the start and finish point. Second, the tiles need some support while the adhesive sets; without it, they may slump down the wall.

The solution is to fix a line of battens across the wall – or right around the room – just above the level of the skirting (baseboard), securing them with partly-driven masonry nails so that they can be removed later when the adhesive has set. The precise level will be dictated by setting-out with the tiling gauge, but will usually be between half and three-quarters of a tile width above the skirting. Do not rely on this being level; it may not be. Draw the line out in pencil first, using the spirit level, and then pin the battens up and check the level again. If everything is straight, it is time to start tiling.

TILING AROUND A DOOR

1 If the door is close to the room corner, start with whole tiles next to the frame. Use a vertical tile guide if the architrave (trim) is not truly vertical.

2 Tile the whole of the main wall area, adding cut tiles next to the room corner and at ceiling level. Remove the tile supports when the adhesive has set.

3 Fit a tile support above the door in line with the tile rows, and another between it and the other room corner, just above skirting (baseboard) level.

TILING AROUND A WINDOW

1 For tiling a wall with a window opening, first decide on where to centre the tiling. On a wall with one window, centre the tiling on a line drawn through its centre.

2 If there are two window openings on a wall, centre the tiles on a line drawn through the centre of each window, provided an exact number of whole tiles will fit between them.

3 Otherwise, centre the tiling on a line drawn midway between the windows. Always work across and up the wall, placing whole tiles up to window-sill level, then up the wall at either side of the window. Then, fit a tile support above the opening to support whole tiles there.

4 Remove the support strips and cut tiles to fit on the face wall at each side and across the top of the window. To tile a window reveal, place whole tiles so they overlap the edges of the tiles on the wall face. Then fill in between these and the frame with cut tiles.

4 Carry on placing whole tiles above the door opening, filling in with cut tiles at the room corner and at ceiling level as in step 2.

5 Remove the tile support above the door opening and fill in all around it with cut and whole tiles as required. Grout the tiles when the adhesive has set.

6 If the door opening is near or at the centre of the room wall, centre the tiling on it and fix tile supports and guide battens (furring strips) as required.

PREPARING THE WALL FOR TILING

The wall surface should be clean and dry. It is possible to tile over painted plaster or plasterboard (gypsum board), but old wall coverings should be removed and brick walls must be rendered. Note that modern tile adhesives allow tiling over existing tiles, so there is no need to remove these if they are securely bonded to the wall surface. There is also no need to fill minor cracks or holes; the tile adhesive will bridge these as it is applied to the wall surface.

When estimating quantities, first select the tile size. Then set out the area to be tiled on the wall and use the setting-out marks to count how many tiles are needed in each horizontal row and each vertical column. Count cut tiles as whole tiles, and then multiply the two figures together to reach the total required. Always add a further 5 per cent to the total to allow for breakages and miscalculations.

MAKING AND USING A TILING GAUGE

1 Use a pencil and one of the chosen tiles to mark up a length of wood for use as a tiling gauge. Allow for the width of tile spacers if using them.

2 Hold the tiling gauge horizontally against the wall to see how many tiles each row will take, and also to centre the tiling on a wall feature or window opening.

3 Similarly, hold the gauge vertically to assess how many tiles will fill each column, and where best to position any cut tiles that may be needed.

MARKING OUT A SPLASHBACK

1 When tiling a small area with rows of whole tiles, use the tiling gauge to mark the extent of the tiled area on the wall. Here each row will have five tiles.

2 Next, use a spirit level to mark a true horizontal base line above which the first row of whole tiles will be fixed. Cut tiles will fit below it.

3 Then use the spirit level again to complete a grid of horizontal and vertical guidelines on the wall surface, ready for a tile support to be fixed.

FITTING TILE SUPPORTS

1 Use masonry pins (tacks) to fix the support to the wall, aligned with the guide line. Drive the pins in only part of the way so that they can be removed later.

2 When tiling large areas or whole walls, pin a vertical guide batten (furring strip) to the wall as well to help keep the tile columns truly vertical.

POSITIONING CUT TILES FOR PANELS

ABOVE If the height of a tiled splashback is determined by a feature such as a mirror or window, position a row of cut tiles along the top of the panel.

ABOVE If the width of the tiling is defined, as with a bath panel, always position cut tiles of equal size at either side.

ESTIMATING QUANTITIES

Tile size	No/sq m	No/sq yd
106 × 106 mm (4¼ × 4¼ in)	86	71
200 × 100 mm (8 × 4 in)	48	41
150 × 150 mm (6 × 6 in)	43	36

TILING PLAIN WALLS

Once all the necessary setting-out work has been done, the actual technique of fixing tiles to walls is quite simple: spread the adhesive and press the tiles into place. However, there must be an adhesive bed of even thickness to ensure that neighbouring tiles sit flush with one another. To obtain this, use a toothed spreader (usually supplied with the tile adhesive; buy one otherwise). Scoop some adhesive from the tub with the spreader, and draw it across the wall with the teeth pressed hard against the plaster to leave ridges of a standard height on the wall. Apply enough adhesive to fix about ten or twelve tiles at a time.

Bed the tiles into the adhesive with a pressing and twisting motion, aligning the first tile with the vertical guideline or batten (furring strip). If using tile spacers, press one into the adhesive next to the top corner of the first tile, and place the second one in the row. Carry on placing spacers and tiles until the end of the row is reached.

Add subsequent rows in the same way until all the whole tiles are in place. It is now time to tackle any cut tiles that are needed at the ends of the rows, and along the base of the tiled area beneath the horizontal tile support. Remove this, and the tile spacers, only when the adhesive has set; allow 24 hours.

FIXING WHOLE TILES

1 Use a notched spreader to scoop some adhesive from the tub and spread it on the wall. Press the teeth against the wall to leave ridges of even height.

2 Place the first tile on the tile support, with its side edge against the pencilled guideline or vertical guide batten (furring strip) as appropriate.

3 Add a tile spacer against the tile corner and place the second tile. Add more tiles to complete the row, then build up succeeding rows in the same way.

CUTTING TILES

1 Use a pencil-type tile cutter and a straightedge to make straight cuts. Measure and mark the tile width needed and score a line across the glaze.

2 Place a nail or matchstick (wooden match) under the scored line at each side of the tile, and break it with downward hand pressure on each half of the tile.

USING A TILE-CUTTING JIG

1 For making angled cuts as well as straight ones, a tile-cutting jig is invaluable. To set it up, first fix the side fence to the angle required.

2 Then draw the slide-mounted cutting point across the tile while holding it firmly in place with the other hand. Take care to score the tile only once.

3 Finally snap the tile along the scored line by holding the tile against the guide bars and lowering the cutter handle with its tip under the tile.

COMPLETING THE WALL

1 Measure, mark and cut the sections of tile needed to complete each row of tiling. Spread a little adhesive over their backs and press them into place.

2 When tiling adjacent walls, place all the cut pieces on the first wall. Repeat the operation on the second wall, overlapping the original cut pieces.

3 When tiling external corners, always set out the tiles so that whole tiles meet on the corner. Overlap the tiles as shown.

3 Use a cutting guide or tiling jig if preferred, especially for cutting narrow strips. This type holds the tile securely and also guides the tile cutter accurately.

4 The traditional way of making a cutout in a tile is to score its outline on the tile and then to gradually nibble away the waste material with pincers.

5 An alternative is to use a special abrasive-coated tile saw. This is indispensable for making internal cutouts – to fit around pipes, for example.

When all the tiles are in place, including any cut tiles that are required, it is time to tackle the final stage of the job – filling in the joint lines between the tiles with grout. This can be bought in powder form or ready-mixed; the latter is more convenient to use, but a little more expensive. Use a flexible spreader (usually supplied with the grout) to force it into the gaps, a damp sponge or cloth to remove excess grout from the face of the tiles, and a short length of wooden dowel or similar material to smooth the grout lines. A clean, dry cloth is needed to polish the tiles afterwards.

Alternative edging techniques

Most ceramic wall tiles have two glazed edges, making it possible to finish off an area of tiling or an external corner with a glazed edge exposed. However, there are alternative ways of finishing off tiling. It can be edged with wooden mouldings or plastic trim strips.

Wooden mouldings can be bedded into the tile adhesive on walls; to edge worktops they can be pinned (tacked) or screwed to the worktop edge.

Plastic edge and corner mouldings (nosings) have a perforated flange which is bedded in the tile adhesive before the tiles are placed. These mouldings come in a range of pastel and bright primary colours to complement or contrast with the tiling.

GROUTING THE TILES

1 Apply the grout to the tile joints by drawing the loaded spreader across them at right angles to the joint lines. Scrape off excess grout and reuse it.

2 Use a damp sponge or cloth to wipe the surface of the tiles before the grout dries out. Rinse it out in clean water from time to time.

3 Then use a short length of wooden dowel or a similar implement to smooth the grout lines to a gently concave cross section.

4 Allow the grout to harden completely, then polish the tiles with a dry cloth to remove any slight remaining bloom and leave them clean and shiny.

1 Bed plastic edge or corner trim into the adhesive, then position the tiles so that they fit flush against the curved edge of the trim strip.

2 As an alternative to plastic, use wooden mouldings bedded in the tile adhesive. Here an L-shaped moulding forms a neat external corner trim.

3 When tiling over existing tiles, some way of disguising the double thickness along exposed edges will be needed. A quadrant (quarter-round) moulding is ideal.

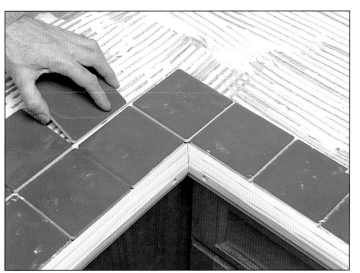

4 Wood can be used to edge a tiled counter top. Start by attaching the moulding to the edge of the worktop so it will fit flush with the tiled surface.

5 Spread the tile adhesive and bed the tiles in place, checking that they lie level with the top edge of the moulding and flush with each other.

6 Plug the counterbored screw holes by gluing in short lengths of dowel and chiselling them off flush with the moulding. Finally, grout the tile joints.

TILING

USING MOSAICS AND CORK TILES

Small mosaic tiles are an attractive alternative to square or rectangular tiles, especially for small areas of tiling where their size will look particularly appropriate. Modern mosaic tiles come in a range of shapes and sizes, from simple squares and roundels to interlocking shapes such as hexagons. They are generally sold in sheets backed with an open-mesh cloth that holds the individual mosaic pieces at the correct spacing and greatly speeds up the installation process, since the entire sheet is stuck to the wall in one go. If cut pieces are needed to fill in the perimeter of the tiled area, simply cut individual mosaic tiles from the sheet with scissors, trim them to size with a tile cutter and position them one by one. Mosaic tiles are fixed and grouted with ordinary tiling products.

One other type of wall tile is popular as a wall covering. Cork tiles are made by compressing the bark of the cork tree into blocks, and then slicing them up into squares – 300 mm (12 in) is the commonest size – or rectangles. They come in a range of natural shades, and may also be stained or printed with surface designs during manufacture. They are stuck to the wall surface with a special water-based contact adhesive, and since they are virtually impossible to remove once placed, they should be regarded as a long-term decorative option and their use carefully planned beforehand.

TIP

If using cork tiles on walls, change the faceplate screws on light switches and socket outlets (receptacles) for longer ones; the originals will be too short to reach the lugs in the mounting box.

USING MOSAIC TILES

1 Start by putting up a horizontal tile support and a vertical tiling guide, as for ordinary tiling. Then apply an area of tile adhesive to the wall.

2 Position the first sheet of mosaic tiles on the wall, in the angle between the tiling support and the tiling guide, and press it firmly into place.

USING CORK TILES

1 To ensure that the tile rows and columns build up correctly, draw horizontal and vertical pencil guidelines on the wall. Place the first tile.

2 If border tiles are to be cut, hold a whole tile over the last whole tile fixed, butt another against the frame and mark its edge on the tile underneath it.

3 After placing several sheets, use a mallet and a piece of plywood to tamp the mosaics down evenly. Use a towel or a thin carpet offcut as a cushion. Ensure the grouting spaces between each sheet are equal.

4 To fill in the perimeter of the area, snip individual mosaic tiles from the sheet, cut them to the size required and bed them in the adhesive.

5 Spread grout over the tiled area, working it well into the gaps between the individual mosaics. Wipe off excess grout, and polish the surface when dry.

3 Place the marked tile on a board and cut it with a sharp utility knife. The exposed part of the sandwiched tile in step 2 will fit the border gap precisely.

4 Fit the cut piece of border tile in place on the wall. Shave or sand its cut edge down a fraction if it is a tight fit. Cut and fit others in the same way.

5 To fit a tile around an obstacle such as a light switch, make a paper or card template and test its fit before cutting the actual tile.

6 Run a rolling pin or a length of broom handle over the completed surface to ensure that all the tiles are well bonded to the wall.

SETTING OUT TILED FLOORS

Like tiled walls, tiled floors need careful setting-out if the end result is to look neat and professional. This is especially important with glazed ceramic and quarry tiles and also patterned vinyl and lino tiles, but matters rather less with plain vinyl or cork tiles where the finished effect is of uniform colour and the joints between the tiles are practically invisible.

Fortunately the necessary setting-out is much easier with floor tiles than wall tiles, since the tiles can be dry-laid on the floor surface and moved around until a starting point is found that gives the best arrangement, with cut border tiles of approximately equal size all around the perimeter of the room.

In a regular-shaped room, start by finding the actual centre point of the floor, by linking the midpoints of opposite pairs of walls with string lines. In an irregularly-shaped room, place string lines as shown in the illustration so that they avoid obstructions, and then link the midpoints of opposite pairs of strings to find the room's centre. Now dry-lay rows of tiles out towards the walls in each direction, remembering to allow for the joint thickness if appropriate, to see how many whole tiles will fit in and to check whether this starting point results in over-narrow border tiles or awkward cuts against obstacles. Move the rows slightly to improve the fit if necessary, then chalk the string lines and snap them against the floor surface to mark the starting point.

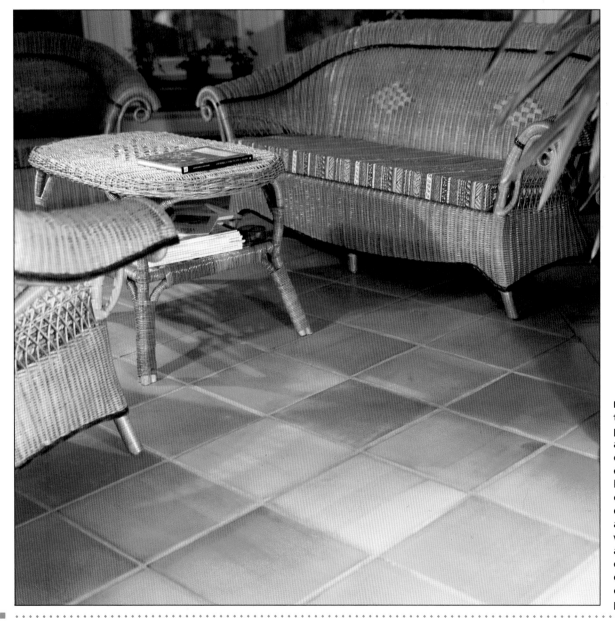

LEFT Quarry and terracotta tiles provide a durable and attractive floor covering and are especially suited to kitchens and conservatories. To ensure that the tiles are correctly aligned with equal borders around the perimeter of the room, it is essential to follow the correct setting-out procedures.

1 In a regular-shaped room, find the room's centre by linking the midpoints of opposite pairs of walls with string lines.

2 In an irregularly shaped room, use string lines that avoid obstacles, and link the midpoints of these as shown to find the centre point.

3 To ensure that tiles will be laid square to the door threshold if the walls are out of square, place a string line at right angles to it across the room to the opposite wall.

4 Place a second string line at right angles to the first so that it passes through the room's centre point.

5 Place a third string line at right angles to the second, again passing through the centre point, to complete the laying guide.

6 Dry-lay rows of tiles out from the centre of the room towards the walls, allowing for the joint width as appropriate to check the width of the border tiles and the fit around any obstacles.

7 Adjust the string lines to get the best possible fit, chalk them and snap them against the floor to mark the laying guidelines.

LAYING CERAMIC FLOOR TILES

Both glazed ceramic and quarry tiles can be laid directly over a concrete floor, as long as it is sound and dry. They can also be laid on a suspended timber floor if it is strong enough to support the not inconsiderable extra weight (check this with a building surveyor). In this case cover the floorboards with exterior-grade plywood, screwed down or secured with annular nails (spiral flooring nails) to prevent it from lifting; this will provide a stable, level base for the tiles.

Glazed ceramic floor tiles are laid with specially formulated adhesive, which should be a waterproof type in bathrooms and a flexible type if tiling on a suspended floor. Quarry and terracotta tiles are laid on mortar over a solid concrete floor, and in thick-bed tile adhesive over plywood.

Old floor coverings should be lifted before laying ceramic or quarry tiles, but if a solid floor is covered with well-bonded vinyl or cork tiles, these can be left in place and tiled over, using tile adhesive. First remove any wax polish used on them.

Set out the floor as described previously, but transfer the starting point to the corner of the room farthest from the door once the setting-out has been completed.

TIP

Remember to take off and shorten room doors before laying floor tiles, and remove enough to allow the door to clear both the plywood underlay and the new tiles.

LAYING CERAMIC FLOOR TILES

1 Pin tiling guides to the floor in the corner of the room at right angles to each other, then spread some adhesive on the floor with a notched-edge trowel.

2 Place the first tile in the angle between the tiling guides, butting it tightly against them and pressing it down firmly into the adhesive bed.

3 As the tiles are laid, use tile spacers to ensure an even gap between them. Use a straightedge to check that all the tiles are horizontal and level.

4 To cut border tiles, lay a whole tile over the last whole tile laid, butt another against the skirting (baseboard) and mark its edge on the tile underneath.

5 Cut the tile and use the exposed part of the sandwiched tile in step 4 to fill the border gap. Use the offcut to fill the next border gap if it is wider than the gap.

6 Use a squeegee to spread grout over the tiles and fill all the joint lines. Wipe excess adhesive from the surface of the tiles with a damp cloth.

7 Use a piece of dowel or a similar rounded implement to smooth the grout lines. Then polish the tile surface with a clean, dry cloth.

LAYING QUARRY TILES

1 Add a third tiling guide to form a bay four tiles wide. Put down a thin mortar bed and place the first row of tiles, using a tiling gauge to space them.

2 Complete four rows of four tiles, then check that they are level. Tamp down any that are proud and lift and rebed any that are lying low.

3 Complete the first bay, then remove the third tiling guide and reposition it another four tile widths away. Fill the second bay with mortar and tamp it down.

4 Complete the second bay in the same way as the first. Continue in this fashion across the room until all the whole tiles are laid.

5 If installing a tiled upstand, place this next, aligning individual units with the floor tiling. Then cut and fit the border tiles.

6 Mix up a fairly dry mortar mix and use a stiff-bristled brush to work it well into the joints between the tiles. Brush away excess mortar while working.

LAYING VINYL, LINO AND CORK FLOOR TILES

Vinyl, lino and cork floor tiles are available in both plain and self-adhesive types. Cork tiles may be unsealed or vinyl-coated. For plain vinyl tiles an emulsion-type latex flooring adhesive is used, while plain cork tiles and lino tiles are best stuck with a water-based contact adhesive; solvent-based types give off fumes that are most unpleasant and are also dangerously flammable. For vinyl-coated cork tiles, use a special vinyl acrylic adhesive.

Since these tiles are comparatively thin, any unevenness in the subfloor will show through the tiles. Cover timber floors with a hardboard underlay first. Concrete floors may need localized repairs or treatment with a self-smoothing compound to give them a smooth finish.

If laying patterned tiles, set the floor out carefully. With plain tiles, setting-out may not appear to be so important, but nevertheless the floor should still be set out carefully to ensure that the tile rows run out at right angles from the room door.

1 If using self-adhesive tiles, simply peel the backing paper off and place the tile in position on the subfloor against the marked guidelines.

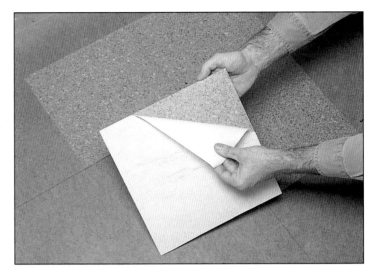

2 Align self-adhesive tiles carefully with their neighbours before sticking them down; the adhesive grabs positively and repositioning may be difficult.

3 If using non-adhesive tiles, spread the appropriate type of adhesive on the subfloor, using a notched spreader to ensure an even thickness.

4 After placing an area of tiles, use a smooth block of wood to work along the joints. This will ensure that they are all well bedded in the adhesive.

5 To cut border tiles, lay a whole tile over the last whole tile laid, butt another against the skirting (baseboard) and mark its edge on the tile underneath.

6 Place the marked tile on a board and cut it with a sharp utility knife. The exposed part of the sandwiched tile in step 5 will fit the border gap perfectly.

7 Fit the cut piece of border tile in place. Trim its edge slightly if it is a tight fit. Mark, cut and fit the other border tiles in exactly the same way.

8 To cut a tile at an external corner, lay a whole tile over the last whole tile in one adjacent row, butt another against the wall and draw along its edge.

9 Move the sandwiched tile to the other side of the corner, again butt the second whole tile against the wall and mark its edge on the sandwiched tile.

10 Use the utility knife to cut out the square waste section along the marked lines, and offer up the L-shaped border tile to check its fit before fixing it.

SEALING CORK TILES

When laying unsealed cork tiles, take care not to get adhesive on the faces of the tiles, and seal the surface with three coats of polyurethane varnish or a proprietary cork sealer to protect the surface from dirt and moisture. If access to the room is necessary while the floor is being sealed, do half the floor one day and the other half the next day.

LAYING FLOOR COVERINGS

The wide range of floor coverings includes carpets, sheet vinyl, and decorative wood panels and strips.

Carpets laid loose have been used on floors for millennia, but it is only a few decades ago that wall-to-wall fitted carpeting became popular. Traditional woven carpets made from natural fibres have been challenged by carpets made from synthetic fibres and by alternative methods of manufacture. There is now a huge choice of colours and patterns in types to suit all locations and wear conditions, available in various widths.

Sheet vinyl floor coverings come in a huge range of colours and patterns, and may also have a surface embossed along the lines of the design to give plausible imitations of other floor coverings such as tiles, marble, wood and cork. Some more expensive types have a cushioned underside formed by incorporating small air bubbles during manufacture, which makes them warmer and softer underfoot than their solid counterparts.

There are two main types of wooden floor covering, wood-block, sometimes called wood mosaic, and wood-strip. The former consists of small slivers of wood (usually a hardwood) laid in groups and stuck to strong cloth to form wooden 'tiles', while the latter is just what its name implies: narrow hardwood planks laid over an existing floor.

OPPOSITE
Fitted carpet is still the most popular choice for living rooms, and the combination of hardwearing fibres and stunning designs now available makes it possible to complement and enhance any style of interior.

FLOORING TOOLS AND EQUIPMENT

For laying *carpet* the basic essentials are a tape measure and a sharp utility knife with a good supply of extra blades for cutting and trimming the carpet to fit. As an alternative, special carpet shears can be used.

For a *woven carpet* a carpet stretcher is invaluable. This is a device with a horizontal pad of metal spikes at one end which is locked into the carpet, and a cushioned pad at the other end which is nudged with the knee to stretch the carpet into place. It is probably best to hire this relatively expensive tool, which will not be needed very often.

Also needed are some carpet gripper strips to hold the carpet in position around the perimeter of the room. Gripper strips are thin strips of plywood fitted with angled nails that grip the underside of the carpet, and they are themselves nailed to the floor about 10 mm (⅜ in) from the skirting (baseboard) all around the room. The edge of the carpet is then tucked down into the gap, usually with a carpet fitter's bolster. A wide brick bolster (stonecutter's) chisel may be used instead, as long as it is clean.

A range of tools for laying carpet, vinyl and wooden floorings include: gripper rods (**1**), a single-sided brass threshold (saddle) strip (**2**), an aluminium carpet-to-vinyl strip (**3**), a threshold cover strip (**4**), a carpet-to-carpet strip (**5**), right-handed (**6**) or left-handed (**7**) carpet shears, a carpet knife with spare blades (**8**), staples (**9**) and a staple hammer (**10**), a recess scriber (**11**), a tack hammer (**12**), a carpet fitter's bolster (**13**), dividers (**14**), an adjustable straightedge (**15**), hessian (burlap) carpet tape (**16**), liquid adhesive (**17**), double-sided tape (**18**), a retractable steel tape measure (**19**), a carpet stretcher (**20**), a tenon saw (**21**), a pad saw (**22**), a coping saw (**23**) and an electric jigsaw (saber saw) (**24**).

LAYING FLOOR COVERINGS

Foam-backed carpet does not need gripper strips. It may be stapled to the floor with a staple gun, or stuck down with double-sided adhesive tape. For both woven and foam-backed types, adhesive seaming tape may also be needed to join sections of carpet together and threshold (saddle) strips to neatly finish the carpeted edge off at door openings.

For laying *sheet vinyl*, again a tape measure and a sharp utility knife are needed. A long steel straightedge will also be invaluable. For bonding the lengths to the floor along edges and seams, use either double-sided tape or bands of liquid adhesive, spread with a toothed spreader. Lastly, a pair of compasses or a scribing block and pencil, plus a shape tracer, are needed to transfer onto the sheet the outlines of the various floor-level obstacles around the edge of the room.

For laying *wood-block* and *wood-strip* floor coverings, the requirements are general woodworking tools, some adhesive and a spreader for wood-block floors, and pins (tacks) or fixing clips for wood-strip floors, plus varnish or sealer if laying an unsealed type.

UNDERLAYS

Lining paper or cloth underlay is recommended for foam-backed carpets as it prevents the foam from sticking to the floor surface. For woven carpets use either a foam or felt underlay: they are available in various grades and should be matched to the carpet being laid. Heavy-duty underlays are recommended for heavy wear areas such as hallways, or where extra insulation is required.

PREPARING WOOD FLOORS

Securing loose boards

For suspended wood floors – boards laid over floor joists – start by lifting the old floor covering and checking that all the boards are securely fixed to their joists, and that they are reasonably flat and level. Loose boards will creak annoyingly when walked on, and raised edges or pronounced warping may show as lines through the new floor covering.

Use either cut nails or large oval-headed nails to secure loose boards. When driving them near known pipe or cable runs, take care not to pierce them; it is best to drive the new nails as close to existing nail positions as possible for safety.

Laying hardboard

Covering the existing boards with a hardboard underlay is an alternative to floor sanding as a way of ensuring a smooth, flat surface ideal for thin sheet floor coverings. Lay the boards in rows with the joints staggered from row to row, and pin them down with hardboard pins driven in at 150 mm

(6 in) spacings. Lay separate strips above known pipe runs.

If preparing to lay glazed ceramic or quarry tiles on a suspended wood floor, put down exterior-grade plywood.

Sanding floors

Where old floorboards are very uneven, or it is planned to leave them exposed but they are badly stained and marked, hire a floor sanding machine. This resembles a cylinder (reel) lawnmower, with a drum to which sheets of abrasive paper are fitted. A bag at the rear collects the sawdust; however, always wear a face mask when sanding floors. Also hire a smaller disc or belt sander for finishing off the room edges.

If necessary, drive any visible nail heads below the surface. Start sanding with coarse abrasive paper, running the machine at 45° to the board direction, then use medium and fine paper in turn with the machine running parallel to the boards. Use the disc or belt sander to tackle the perimeter of the room where the large sander cannot reach.

SECURING FLOORBOARDS

1 Drive in any nails that have lifted due to warping or twisting of the floorboards, and then recess their heads slightly using a nail punch.

2 If nails will not hold the floorboard flat against the joist, drill pilot and clearance holes and use wood screws to secure the board firmly in place.

TIP

When sanding floorboards, always raise the drum at the end of each pass to prevent the abrasives from damaging the boards while the machine is stationary.

LAYING HARDBOARD

1 If hardboard sheets are used as an underlay for a new floor covering, start by punching in any raised nail heads all over the floor.

2 Nail the hardboard sheets to the floorboards at 150 mm (6 in) intervals along the edges and also 300 mm (12 in) apart across the face of each sheet.

SANDING FLOORBOARDS

1 Use a floor sander to smooth and strip old floorboards. Drape the flex (cord) over one shoulder and raise the drum before starting the machine up.

2 Run the machine at 45° to the board direction to start with, first in one direction and then in the other at right angles to the original passes.

3 Then switch to a medium-grade abrasive and run the sander back and forth parallel with the board direction. Finish off with fine-grade abrasive.

4 Use a smaller disc or belt sander to strip areas close to the skirtings (baseboards) and door thresholds, where the larger drum sander cannot reach.

5 Use a scraper to remove paint or varnish from inaccessible areas such as around pipework, then sand the stripped wood smooth by hand.

Ground floors of solid concrete are prone to two main problems: cracking or potholing of the surface, and rising damp caused by a failure in the damp-proof membrane within the floor structure. Cracks and depressions may show through new floor coverings, especially thinner types such as sheet vinyl, while dampness will encourage mould growth beneath the covering.

Relatively narrow cracks can be patched with a repair mortar of 1 part cement to 3 parts sand, or an exterior-quality masonry filler.

If the floor surface is uneven or pitted, it can be covered with a thin layer of self-smoothing compound. There are two types available; both are powders and are mixed with either water or with a special latex emulsion. The mixture is made up in a bucket and poured onto the floor surface, trowelling it out to a thickness of about 3 mm (⅛ in). The liquid finds its own level and dries to give a hard, smooth surface which can be walked on in about 1 hour. Leave it to dry for 24 hours before laying a floor covering over it.

An alternative approach is to cover the concrete with a floating floor of chipboard (particle board), if raising the floor level will not cause problems at door thresholds. The boards can be laid directly on the concrete over heavy-duty polythene (polyethylene) sheeting, which acts as a vapour barrier. If additional insulation is required, put down polystyrene boards first and then lay the new flooring over them.

Treat damp floors immediately with one or two coats of a proprietary damp-proofing liquid.

LAYING A SELF-SMOOTHING COMPOUND

1 Start by sweeping the floor clear of dust and debris. Then scrub away any patches of grease from the surface with strong detergent solution.

2 Key the surface of vinyl floor tiles by sanding it before laying the compound. Wipe away the dust with a damp cloth.

3 If the concrete surface is very dusty or appears unduly porous, seal it by brushing on a generous coat of diluted PVA building adhesive (white general-purpose adhesive).

4 Mix up the self-smoothing compound in a bucket, following the manufacturer's instructions carefully to ensure that the mix is the right consistency and free from lumps.

5 Starting in the corner farthest from the room door, pour the compound out onto the floor surface to cover an area of about 1 sq m (11 sq ft).

6 Use a plasterer's trowel to smooth the compound out to a thickness of about 3 mm (⅛ in). Mix, pour and level further batches as required.

LAYING A CHIPBOARD FLOOR

1 You can level and insulate a concrete floor by laying a floating floor of chipboard (particle board) over it. Put down heavy-duty polythene (polyethylene) sheets first.

2 Tape the sheet to the walls; it will be hidden behind the new skirting (baseboard) later. Then butt-joint 25 mm (1 in) polystyrene insulation boards.

3 Cover the insulation with tongued-and-grooved flooring-grade boards. Use cut pieces as necessary, and add a tapered threshold (saddle) strip at the door.

REMOVING OLD FLOOR COVERINGS

Generally speaking, old floor coverings should always be lifted before laying new ones. This also provides an opportunity to inspect the floor itself and to carry out any repairs that may be necessary. However, there are some situations where it may not be practical or necessary to lift an existing floor covering – for example, where vinyl tiles have been laid over a concrete floor and they are firmly stuck to it. Stripping such a large area will be an extremely time-consuming job unless a professional floor tile stripping machine is hired.

1 The backing of old foam-backed carpets may remain stuck to the floor surface. Brush it up, and also remove any remaining staples or seaming tape.

2 To lift vinyl tiles or sheet vinyl that has been stuck along edges and seams, use a heat gun to soften the adhesive and quickly pull up the flooring.

3 If vinyl or cork tiles have been stuck onto a hardboard underlay, lift a few tiles to expose the board edges and then lever the boards up in one piece.

4 Lift wood-block or wood-strip floors if they are damaged or show signs of lifting. Otherwise cover them by pinning on a hardboard overlay.

PAINTING AND VARNISHING FLOORS

Rather than being replaced, floors can simply be brightened up with paint or varnish. This is not only economical, but can create some effects that an off-the-shelf material cannot provide. This technique can be used directly on both solid and wooden floors as long as the surface is in good condition. If it is not, cover floorboards with a hardboard overlay, or treat solid floors with a self-smoothing compound.

Concrete floors can be given a smooth, washable and durable finish by using special floor paint. Make sure the surface is clean, dry and free from oil or grease. Then apply the first coat thinned with white spirit (paint thinner) to act as a sealer, and add two further full-strength coats.

Varnishing bare floorboards, especially after they have been stripped with a floor sander, can create a stunning floor that will contrast beautifully with loose-laid rugs. A stain can be applied before the varnish if wanted. Simply prepare the floor in the same way as any other indoor woodwork, repairing any major surface defects and checking that nail heads are well punched down. If using stain, apply sparingly with a cloth along the grain direction and leave it to dry. Apply three coats of clear varnish to seal the surface. Alternatively, use a coloured sealer to do both jobs with one product. Paint can also be used if it is preferred to hide the grain of the wood.

Stencils or other patterns can be applied either direct to the boards or to a hardboard overlay. A tiled effect can be created by putting down hardboard squares that have been decorated with a special paint effect such as marbling. At least three coats of varnish should be applied over any painted effect, or it will soon wear away.

PAINTING CONCRETE FLOORS Seal and decorate concrete floors in areas such as utility rooms by applying a proprietary floor paint with a paint roller on an extension pole.

STAIN EFFECTS Stain and varnish new or stripped floorboards after sanding them smooth and filling any defects. Use a cardboard mask if applying more than one shade.

STENCIL DESIGNS Effects such as stencils can be applied to a stained or painted floor. Mark out the line of the pattern on the floor and stencil on the design.

1 **PAINTING HARDBOARD** Cover poor-quality floorboards with hardboard, laid with the smooth side uppermost, then paint on the chosen design. Use a strip of wood as a guide.

2 Alternatively, use masking tape to outline the design, apply the paint, and remove the tape when the paint is just touch-dry.

3 With any painted effect, allow the paint to dry hard, then seal the floor surface with three coats of clear varnish or floor sealer.

ABOVE Here plain floorboards have been enhanced with a two-colour painted diamond design, an effect that tones well with the simple painted decor.

LAYING FOAM-BACKED CARPET

Laying traditional woven carpet can be difficult for the amateur, because it has to be correctly tensioned across the room by using gripper strips and a carpet stretcher if it is to wear well. Because of the cost of such carpet, it may be considered best to leave the job to professionals. However, there is no reason why the do-it-yourselfer should not get some practice by laying less expensive foam-backed carpet in, for example, a spare bedroom. It is possible to disguise any slight inaccuracies that creep into the cutting and fitting process more easily here than with smooth sheet floor coverings such as vinyl, so the job is a good introduction to the general technique of laying roll floor coverings.

Start by putting down a paper or cloth underlay on the floor, taping the joins and stapling the underlay down so that it cannot creep as work continues. Unroll the carpet across the room, with the excess lapping up the walls. Roughly trim the excess all around the room, leaving 50 mm (2 in) for final trimming. Make small cuts at external corners such as around chimney breasts (fireplace projections), and let the tongues fall back into alcoves, then trim off the waste across the face of the chimney breast. Next, press the carpet into internal corners and mark the corner point with a finger. Make cuts to remove the triangle of carpet from the internal angle. Finally, trim the perimeter with a knife drawn along the angle between skirting (baseboard) and wall, and secure the edges with double-sided adhesive tape. Fit a threshold (saddle) strip across door openings.

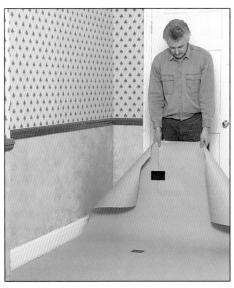

1 Before laying a foam-backed carpet, put down a paper or cloth underlay to keep the foam from sticking to the floor. Tape joins and staple it in place.

2 Put double-sided adhesive tape all around the perimeter of the room, then unroll the carpet and position it so that it laps up the room walls.

3 Butt the edge of the carpet up against the longest straight wall in the room. Peel the backing paper off the tape and bed the edge into place.

4 Work the carpet across the floor to the opposite wall to ensure that it is lying flat. Then trim that edge against the skirting (baseboard) and tape it down too.

5 Make cuts at internal and external corners in order to bed the carpet onto the tape. Trim excess carpet by drawing a knife along the angle. Take care not to over-trim.

6 Use adhesive seaming tape to join pieces of carpet together where necessary in particularly large rooms. Pressure from a wallpaper seam roller ensures a good bond.

LAYING CARPET TILES

Carpet tiles are among the simplest floor coverings to lay, because they are highly tolerant of any slight inaccuracy in cutting to fit. The cheapest types are usually plain in colour and have a very short pile or a corded appearance, while more expensive tiles may have a longer pile and are available in patterns as well as plain colours. Most are designed to be loose-laid, with just the edges and door thresholds (saddles) secured with bands of adhesive or double-sided tape. This makes it easy to lift individual tiles for cleaning or to even out wear.

Most carpet tiles are marked on the back with an arrow to indicate the pile direction. Align these for a plain effect, or lay them at right angles to create a chequerboard effect. When satisfied with the layout, lift perimeter tiles and put down double-sided tape all around the room. Peel the backing paper off the top of the tape and press the tiles into place. Finish doorways with a threshold (saddle) strip.

CUTTING CARPET TILES

1 Cut carpet tiles from the back on a cutting board, using a sharp utility knife and a steel straightedge, after measuring the size of the cut tile required and marking the tile back.

2 After cutting cleanly through the backing, separate the two halves and lay the cut tile in place. Trim any frayed pile off with scissors.

LAYING WOVEN CARPET

The laying and trimming technique used for laying woven carpets is broadly similar to that described for foam-backed carpets, with two main exceptions: the edges are secured on toothed gripper strips instead of by double-sided adhesive tape, and the carpet must be tensioned across the room to ensure that it wears evenly and cannot ruck up in use.

Start by nailing the gripper strips to the floor all around the room, using a hardboard or cardboard spacer to set them about 10 mm (⅜ in) away from the skirtings (baseboards). Then put down a good-quality foam underlay, paper side up, cutting it to fit just inside the gripper strips. Tape any joins and staple the underlay to the floor at regular intervals.

Now unroll the carpet, trim it roughly and make small diagonal cuts at internal and external corners. Use a carpet fitter's bolster or a clean brick bolster (stonecutter's chisel) to press one edge of the carpet down onto the gripper strips, then trim off excess carpet and use the bolster to tuck the carpet edge into the gap between the strips and the wall.

Use the carpet stretcher to tension the carpet along the adjacent walls and across the room, hooking it onto the gripper strips as each section is stretched. Trim the other walls too, and finally fit the carpet neatly into the doorway, securing it with a threshold (saddle) strip.

1 Nail gripper strips all around the perimeter of the room, using a spacer to set them slightly away from the skirting (baseboard).

2 Lay underlay, trimmed to butt up to the gripper strips. Tape pieces together as necessary, then staple the underlay to the floor at intervals.

3 Unroll the carpet and trim it roughly all around. Then make cuts at external corners so that tongues of carpet will fit around them.

4 Press one edge of the carpet onto the gripper strips with a carpet fitter's bolster to ensure that the angled teeth grip the carpet backing securely.

5 Cut off the excess carpet along this edge by running a sharp utility knife along the angle between the gripper strip and the skirting, as shown.

6 Use the blade of the bolster to tuck the trimmed edge of the carpet into the angle between strip and the skirting. Then tension the carpet along adjacent walls.

7 Make release cuts at internal corners too, then trim the waste along the other walls of the room as before and tuck the cut edges into the perimeter gap.

8 At door frames and similar obstacles, trim the carpet to follow the contours of the obstacle as closely as possible, and press it onto the gripper strip.

STRETCHING CARPET

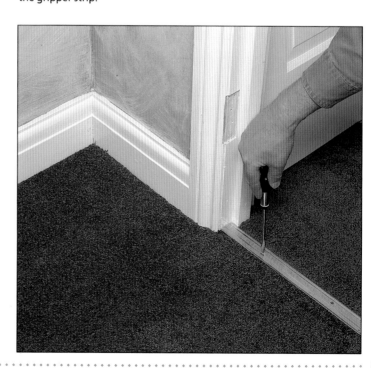

Stretch a carpet along two adjacent walls of the room, hooking it onto the gripper strips. Then stretch it across the room first in one direction, then in the other.

9 Complete the installation by fitting a door threshold (saddle) strip. Different types are available for linking carpet to carpet and carpet to smooth floor coverings.

LAYING STAIR CARPET

The technique of carpeting a flight of stairs is similar in principle to that used for carpeting a room, with gripper strips being used to hold the carpet to the treads. The job is easiest on a straight flight, but it is not too difficult to cope with winding flights or projecting bullnose steps because cuts can be made across the carpet at any point on the flight and the joins hidden neatly at the back of the tread.

Start by nailing on the gripper strips just above the bottom edge of each riser and just in front of the rear edge of each tread. The space between them should be about the same as the thickness of a single fold of the carpet. Instead of two lengths of the normal plywood-based strip, special one-piece L-section metal grippers can be used here. Add short lengths of ordinary gripper strip to the sides of the treads, the thickness of the carpet away from the sides of the flight. Next, cut pieces of underlay to cover each tread and the face of the riser below, and fix them in position with a staple gun or carpet tacks.

Start laying the carpet at the top of the flight. If the same carpet is being used on the landing, this should be brought over the edge of the top step and down the face of the first riser. Therefore the top edge of the stair carpet should be tucked into the gripper strips at the bottom of the first riser. Trim the edges of the carpet on the first tread, then on the next riser, and tuck them in before locking the fold of carpet into the gripper strips at the back of the next tread with a carpet fitter's bolster. Continue in this way to the bottom of the flight, where the stair carpet finishes at the base of the first riser whether or not the floor below uses the same carpet.

1 Cut lengths of gripper strip to fit across the width of the flight, and nail them in position at the foot of each riser and also at the back of each tread.

2 Next, cut and fit a short length of gripper strip to the side of each tread. Position them just less than the carpet thickness away from the sides of the flight.

3 Cut pieces of underlay to fit between each tread/riser angle, and staple or tack them in place so they fit smoothly over the nosing at the front of the tread.

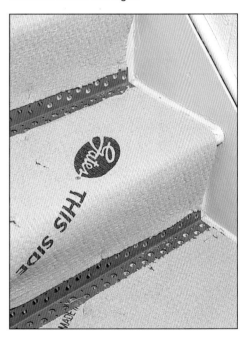

4 As an alternative to using two lengths of plywood gripper strip in the tread/riser angle, fit a one-piece L-section metal strip there instead.

5 Start fitting the carpet at the top of the flight, trimming each tread and riser in turn and then forcing a fold of carpet into the angled gripper strips.

6 On an open-string staircase, either trim the carpet to fit around each baluster or fold over the edge and tack it to fit against the baluster as shown here.

7 On winder (curved) stairs, cut a piece of carpet to cover each tread and the riser beneath it. Align it so that the weave is at right angles to the riser.

8 Secure each piece of carpet to the gripper strip at the rear of the tread first, then stretch it over the tread and down to the next gripper strip.

9 Trim off the waste from the bottom edge of the riser, then repeat the cutting and fitting sequence for any other winder steps on the flight.

10 If the flight finishes with a projecting bullnose step, trim and tack the carpet to the riser as shown and cover the riser with a separate strip.

ALTERNATIVE FIXINGS

1 When fitting a stair runner rather than a full-width carpet, paint or stain the stair treads and anchor the carpet with stair rods.

2 If you are using foam-backed carpet on your stairs, fit special gripper strips for foam-backed carpet into the angles between treads and risers.

LAYING SHEET VINYL

Sheet vinyl flooring can be difficult to lay because it is wide and comparatively stiff to handle, and edge cutting must be done accurately if gaps are not to be noticeable against skirtings (baseboards). Lengths of quadrant beading (a base shoe) can be pinned (tacked) around the perimeter of the room to disguise any serious mistakes.

Most rooms contain at least one long straight wall, and it is often easiest to butt one edge of the vinyl up against this first of all. Use a block of wood and a pencil to scribe the wall profile onto the vinyl and cut along this line for a perfect fit. Alternatively, simply press the vinyl into the angle between wall and floor and cut along it with the knife held at a 45° angle. Then press the ends of the length neatly against the walls at right angles to the first wall, make small diagonal cuts at internal and external angles, and trim the edges to fit there. Finally stick down the edges and any seams with double-sided adhesive tape. Finish off doorways with proprietary threshold (saddle) strips.

1 Unless the wall is perfectly straight, make a cut at the corner and trim the adjacent edges of the sheet with a sharp knife along the angle of wall and floor.

2 At door architraves (trims), make cuts into the edge of the sheet down to floor level so the sheet will lie flat, and trim off the tongues.

3 Use a similar technique for trimming the sheet around larger obstacles such as washbasin pedestals.

4 To join sheet vinyl edge to edge, overlap the two sheets so that the pattern matches and cut through both layers against a steel straightedge. Discard the waste strips.

5 Place a strip of double-sided tape underneath the joint line, peel off the backing paper and press the two cut edges firmly down onto the tape.

6 To fit the sheet around plumbing pipework, make a cut into it at the pipe position and then trim out a circle of the material to fit around it.

7 At door openings, fit a threshold (saddle) strip to anchor the edge of the sheet. Here an existing strip has been prised up and is being hammered down again.

Sheet vinyl flooring is ideal for kitchens with its easy-to-clean surface. The cushioned types also offer extra warmth and softness underfoot.

LAYING WOOD MOSAIC FLOORING

The least expensive way of getting a decorative timber floor finish is by laying mosaic floor tiles, which are square tiles made up from a number of small fingers of decorative hardwood mounted on a cloth or felt backing sheet. This acts as an underlay as well as bonding the fingers together; the result is a sheet that will bend along the joint lines, and so can be easily cut to size if required. Alternatively, the fingers may be wired or stuck together to produce a rigid tile. In either case, tiles are generally either 300 mm (12 in) or 450 mm (18 in) square.

The fingers themselves may be solid wood or veneer on a cheaper softwood backing, and are usually arranged in a basketweave pattern; however, other patterns are also available. A wide range of wood types is used, including mahogany, teak, oak, iroko and merbau. Some tiles are supplied sealed, while others have to be varnished or sealed after being laid.

Laying wood-block floor tiles is a comparatively straightforward job, similar to any other floor tiling project in terms of preparation and setting-out. Store the panels unpacked in the room where they will be laid for at least seven days, to allow them to acclimatize to indoor temperature and humidity levels. This will help to reduce shrinkage or expansion after the tiles are laid. However, an expansion gap should always be left around the perimeter of the room.

1 Find the starting point in the same way as for other kinds of tile. Mark tiling guidelines on the floor and spread some adhesive in the first quarter.

2 Align the first tile carefully with the tiling guidelines and press it firmly down into the adhesive. Bed it down with a hammer and a wood offcut.

3 Lay the next panel in the same way, butting it up against its neighbour. Wipe off any adhesive from the tile faces immediately.

4 To cut edge pieces, lay a whole tile over the last whole tile laid and butt another on top against the skirting (baseboard). Draw along its edge on the middle tile.

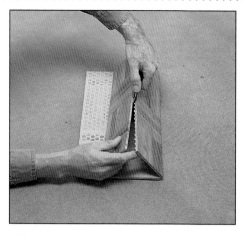

5 The tile can be bent along the main joint lines, and then sections can be separated by cutting through the backing fabric with a sharp utility knife.

6 More complicated cuts running across the fingers of wood can be made with a tenon saw, using very light pressure to avoid splitting or tearing the thin strips.

7 At door architraves (trims) and other similar obstacles, make a paper template or use a proprietary shape tracer to mark the tile. Cut the outline with a coping saw.

8 Cover the cut edges of the tiles by pinning lengths of quadrant beading (a base shoe) to the skirtings. Alternatively, use cork expansion strips along the edges.

9 On new work, do not fix the skirtings until the flooring has been laid. They will then hide the expansion gap.

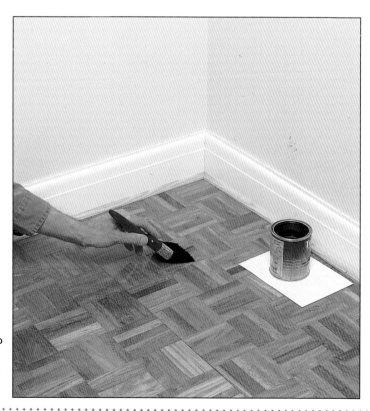

10 Sweep and dust unsealed panels, then apply two or three coats of clear varnish or floor sealer, sanding the surface lightly between coats.

ACCESS HATCHES

If there is a need for access to electrical fittings or pipe runs below the floor, make small hatches so that a whole tile plus the hatch cover can be lifted if necessary. Screw the tile and cover down onto the base floor with wood screws.

LAYING WOOD-STRIP FLOORING

Wood-strip flooring is available in two main types: as solid planks, and as laminated strips (rather like plywood) with a decorative surface veneer. Lengths range from as little as 400 mm (16 in) up to 1800 mm (6 ft), and widths from 70 mm (2¾ in) up to around 200 mm (8 in). Solid planks are usually about 15 mm (⅝ in) thick; laminated types are a little thinner.

Both types are generally tongued-and-grooved on their long edges for easy fitting. Some are designed to be fixed to a wooden subfloor by secret nailing; others are loose-laid, using ingenious metal clips to hold adjacent strips together.

A wide range of wood varieties is available in each type. Laminated types are generally pre-finished; solid types may also be, but some need sealing once they have been laid.

All the hard work involved in putting down wood-strip flooring lies in the preparation; the actual laying, like so many decorating jobs, is simple and proceeds gratifyingly quickly.

Always unpack the strips and leave them in the room where they will be laid for about a week to acclimatize to the temperature and humidity levels in the home. This will help to avoid buckling due to expansion, or shrinkage due to contraction, when laid.

If the manufacturer recommends the use of a special underlay – which may be polythene (polyethylene) sheeting, glass fibre matting or foam – put this down next, and tape or staple the joins together so they do not ruck up while the floor is laid.

1 Make sure that the subfloor is clean, dry and level. Then unroll the special cushioned underlay across the floor, taping one end to keep it in place.

2 Prepare all the lengths of board by hammering the special metal joint clips into the groove on the underside of the boards, next to the tongued edge.

3 Lay the first length, clips outwards, against the wall, using spacers to create an expansion gap next to the wall. Glue the ends of butt-jointed lengths.

4 Position the second row of boards, tapping them together with a hammer and an offcut so the clips on the first row engage in the groove of the second.

5 The last board is fitted without clips. Cut it to width, allowing for the spacers as in step 3, and apply adhesive along its grooved edge.

6 Insert some protective packing against the wall before levering the strip into place. Tamp it down level with a hammer and protect the floor with a board offcut.

7 Replace skirtings (baseboards) or pin (tack) on lengths of quadrant beading (a base shoe) to hide the expansion gap. Weight the board down so it fits tightly against the floor.

8 To fit a board around a pipe, mark its position and drill a suitably sized hole. Then cut out a tapered wedge which can be glued back after fitting the board.

ABOVE Hardwearing and elegant, wood-strip flooring is a practical choice for living rooms, especially if teamed with scatter rugs.

FEATURES AND FITTINGS

A bare room with its areas of flat and featureless plasterwork is a blank canvas which can be embellished in many different ways. Paint and wall coverings obviously play their part, but there is also a wide range of other features which can be added to the room to give it its own personality. The majority, while often decorative in their own right, serve a highly practical function as well.

Wooden mouldings can be fitted to protect the fragile plaster surfaces. These include skirtings (baseboards) fitted around the walls at floor level, and architraves (trims) around flush door and window openings. The right choice of fittings – handles, catches and so on – for the doors and windows, can complete the look of a room. Picture rails allow pictures and mirrors to be hung anywhere without having to

make new fixings. There is a huge range of products to choose from in all these categories.

Finding suitable storage space around the house for all the personal and household belongings every family accumulates can be quite a challenge. The solution is to tailor-make storage to suit its purpose. The storage that is needed can be provided in one of two ways. One is to buy or make pieces of freestanding furniture that match the required storage function. The other is to create built-in storage space – arrays of shelving in alcoves and so on. The former is the best solution for those who value furniture more than function, since the pieces can be moved from one house to another. However, built-in storage is generally more effective in providing the most space for the least money, since the house walls can often be used as part of the structure.

OPPOSITE
The decoration of wall, ceiling and floor
surfaces sets the tone for any colour scheme,
but it is the fixtures and fittings – the extra
touches such as decorative mouldings, door and
window furniture, even pictures and mirrors –
that give a room its individual look.

Trim mouldings are both practical and decorative. They are used as skirtings (baseboards) to protect wall surfaces at floor level from accidental damage, and around door and window openings as architraves (trims) which frame the opening and disguise the joint between the frame and the wall surface. Both can be plain or ornate, and can be painted, stained or varnished. They may need replacing if they are damaged or simply look unfashionable.

Skirtings are often fixed directly to masonry walls with large cut nails in older homes, or with masonry nails in more recent ones. Alternatively, they may be nailed to rough timber fixing blocks or grounds (furrings) which are themselves nailed to the masonry. Boards fixed to blocks are much easier to remove than those nailed direct to the wall, since both cut and masonry nails can have a ferocious grip. In the latter situation it is often easier to

punch the nails through the boards and into the walls than to try to prise them out. Boards on wood-framed walls are simply nailed to the frame, and so are easy to remove.

Architraves are pinned (tacked) in place to the edges of the door or window frame. It is an easy job to prise the trims away with a bolster (stonecutter's) chisel without causing undue damage to the frame or the surrounding wall surface.

REPLACING SKIRTINGS (BASEBOARDS)

1 To replace a small area of damaged board, prise it away from the wall slightly, wedge it and use a tenon saw and mitre box to cut out a section.

2 Nail small support blocks behind the cut ends of the board, using masonry nails on solid walls, and then nail the cut ends to the support blocks.

3 Cut a piece of replacement board to fit, with its ends mitred to match the cutout section. Use plain wood if the skirting profile cannot be matched.

4 Nail the replacement board to the support blocks. If using plain wood, pin (tack) on decorative mouldings to build up a close match to the existing board.

5 When replacing whole lengths, use mitre joints at external corners. Fix the first length, then mark the inside of the mitre on the back of the next board.

6 Cut the mitre joints with a power saw with an adjustable sole plate. Set the cutting angle to just under 45° to ensure that the joint will fit well.

7 At internal corners, fit the first length right into the corner. Then scribe its profile onto the second board; cut this with a coping saw, and fit it.

REPLACING ARCHITRAVES (TRIMS)

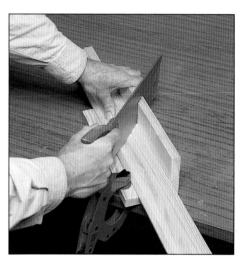

1 Prise off the old mouldings. They should come away easily. If necessary, lever against a block to avoid damaging the surface of the wall.

2 Hold an upright against the frame so that the inside of the mitre joint can be marked on it. Repeat for the other upright.

3 Cut the end of the moulding, using a mitre block or box. Alternatively, mark the line across the moulding with a protractor or combination square.

4 Fix the uprights to the frame by driving in nails at 300 mm (12 in) intervals. Recess the heads with a nail punch and fill the holes later.

5 Hold the top piece above the two uprights to mark the position for the mitre cut at each end. Make the cuts as before and test the piece for fit.

6 Nail the top piece to the frame, checking that the mitre joints are accurately aligned. Then drive a nail through each corner to secure the joint.

DOOR AND WINDOW HARDWARE

Door and window fittings can be ornamental as well as practical and secure. The simplest type of door catch is a spring-loaded ball which is recessed into the door edge. The ball engages in a recess in the door frame as the door is pushed closed, and retracts as the door is pulled open.

A more positive action is provided by a mortise latch; this is also recessed into the door edge and has a projecting bolt which is flat on one face and curved on the other. As the door is pushed shut, the curved face hits the striking plate on the door frame and pushes the bolt back into the latch body. When the door is fully closed the bolt springs out into the recess in the striking plate, with its flat face providing a positive latching action. Turning the door handle rotates a spindle, withdrawing the bolt from the striking plate and allowing the door to open again. A mortise lock combines the same latch mechanism with a lockable bolt.

The commonest items of hardware used on hinged windows are a rotating cockspur handle that is used simply to fasten the window, and a casement stay which props it open in one of several different positions. On sliding sash windows, the basic hardware is a catch that locks the two sashes together when they are closed.

TIP

If fitting lockable window catches and stays, do not leave the keys in the locks in case they fall out as the window is opened and closed. Instead, hang them on a pin driven into the window frame. This also ensures that they are readily available if the window has to be opened in an emergency.

FITTING A MORTISE LATCH

1 To fit a mortise latch to a new door, use the latch body to mark the mortise position on the door edge, in line with the centre rail or lock block.

2 Set a mortise gauge to a setting just wider than the thickness of the latch body, and scribe the outline of the mortise centred on the door edge.

3 Use a flat wood bit in a power drill to make a series of holes between the guidelines, a little deeper than the length of the latch body.

4 Chop out the waste with a chisel and mallet, then pare down the sides of the mortise and clean out the recess. Try the latch for fit in the mortise.

5 Draw around the latch faceplate on the edge of the door, then cut around the lines with a chisel and make a series of parallel cuts across the grain.

6 Carefully chisel out the waste wood between the marked guidelines, taking care not to let the chisel slip and cut beyond the ends of the recess.

7 Hold the latch body against the face of the door in line with the mortise and with its faceplate flush with the door edge. Mark the spindle position.

8 Clamp a piece of scrap wood to the other side of the door. Drill a hole big enough to accept the spindle through the door into the scrap wood.

9 Slide the latch into place in its mortise and make pilot holes through the faceplate with a bradawl. Then drive in the faceplate fixing screws.

10 Insert the spindle and fit a handle onto each end of it. Check that the spindle rotates freely, then screw both the handles to the door.

11 Close the door in order to mark where the latch bolt meets the frame. Then chisel out the recesses for the bolt and striking plate, and screw on the plate.

FITTING A WINDOW HANDLE AND STAY

1 Decide where the cockspur handle should go on the casement and make pilot holes through it with a bradawl. Then screw the handle to the casement.

2 Fit the striking plate to the frame so the cockspur will engage in it. Drill out the frame to a depth of about 20 mm (¾ in) through the slot in the plate.

3 Fit the casement stay by screwing its baseplate to the bottom rail of the casement about one-third of the way along from the hinged edge.

4 Open the window to find the right position for the pins on the frame. Attach the pins, then fit the stay rest on the casement rail.

However beautifully walls are decorated, they will still look rather featureless unless they are brightened up by hanging some pictures, and perhaps a mirror or too as well. Apart from their obvious function, mirrors can make a room seem brighter by reflecting light from the window.

For hanging pictures there is a choice of using individual supports for each picture, or hanging them from a picture rail. Individual supports range from small plastic or metal picture hooks, which are simply nailed to the wall, to heavy-duty fixings attached with screws – and wall plugs on masonry walls. The choice depends solely on the weight of the picture. Use single-pin picture hooks for pictures with a slimline frame up to around 600 mm (2 ft) in either dimension, and a two-pin hook for anything of similar size in a heavy frame. Use two hooks, one at each side of the frame, for pictures up to about 900 mm (3 ft) across, and switch to a screw-in hook for anything larger. With picture rails, the standard S-shaped hooks will support reasonable weights.

Mirrors can be hung like pictures as long as the fixing is strong enough to take the weight. Otherwise they can be secured directly to the wall with special mirror clips. If they have pre-drilled holes at the corners they can be fixed with screws – ideally, mirror screws with special domes or clip-on covers (rosette fastenings).

MIRROR FIXINGS

1 Mirrors can be fixed with pre-drilled holes, using screws plus special washers and spacers that cushion the mirror and allow air circulation.

2 Mark and drill the fixing holes, then thread the screw through the washer, the mirror and the rear spacer before driving the screw. Do not overtighten it.

3 The screw head should just start to compress the washer. Cover it with a screw-on dome (rosette fastening) if using mirror screws, or with a plastic cover otherwise.

4 If using mirror clips, first draw a guideline on the wall where the bottom of the mirror will go, and fit the fixed bottom clips at each end.

5 Set the bottom edge of the mirror in the bottom clips, checking that it is truly level, and mark the wall to indicate where its top edge will be.

6 Screw the slotted top clips to the wall so their top edges are just above the line. Raise them, set the mirror in place, and press the top clips down.

PICTURE FIXINGS

1 Traditional brass picture hooks come in one-pin and two-pin versions. The holes in the hook guide the pin in at an angle to the wall for a firmer fixing.

2 Small plastic picture hooks have three or four short pins to help locate the hook, and are secured by a longer pin driven through the centre hole.

3 A picture rail allows pictures to be hung in any position and at any height. Simply place the hook over the rail and hang the picture wire over it.

FITTING FIXED SHELVING

Wall-mounted shelving is one of two basic types – fixed or adjustable. With fixed shelving, each shelf is supported independently of others using two or more shelf brackets, which are fixed to the wall and to the underside of the shelf itself. With adjustable shelving, the shelves are carried on brackets, studs or tongues which are slotted or clipped into vertical support strips screwed to the wall.

Fixed brackets are ideal for putting up a single shelf – over a radiator, for example – although they can equally well be used to support several shelves. They come in many styles, shapes and colours. Metal brackets are the most usual, but wooden ones in various finishes are also available.

Shelves can be of natural wood or manufactured boards. Ready-made shelves can be bought from do-it-yourself stores; they are usually made of veneered or plastic-coated chipboard (particle board). The latter traditionally have either a white or imitation woodgrain finish, but subtle pastel shades and bold primary colours are becoming more widely available. Otherwise shelves can be cut from full-sized boards: chipboard, plywood, MDF (medium-density fibreboard) and blockboard are all suitable.

SHELF SUPPORT STRIP

This is an ingenious support for single shelves. It consists of a specially shaped channel which is screwed to the wall at the required position; then the shelf is simply knocked into place with a soft-faced mallet. The channel grips the shelf securely, and can support surprisingly heavy loads. Various sizes are available.

USING SHELF BRACKETS

1 Select the correct bracket spacing, then attach the shorter arm of each bracket to the underside of the shelf, flush with the rear edge.

2 Fix the shelf to the wall with a screw driven through one bracket, then check that it is horizontal and mark all the remaining screw positions.

3 Let the shelf swing downwards on its first fixing screw, then drill the other holes. Insert plugs for masonry wall fixings if needed.

4 Swing the shelf back up into position and drive in the remaining fixing screws. Tighten them fully so the screw heads pull the brackets against the wall.

USING SHELF SUPPORT STRIPS

1 Hold the support strip against the wall at the desired level, and mark the position of the central screw hole. Drill the hole and attach the strip.

2 Place a spirit level on top of the strip. Swivel the strip until it is precisely level, and mark the positions of the remaining screw holes.

3 Swivel the strip out of the way and drill the other holes. Then secure it with the remaining screws and slot the shelf into place.

4 Small shelf support blocks are also available for mounting small display shelves. The shelf is clamped in place by tightening a locking screw underneath.

RIGHT Individual brackets can be used to mount more than one shelf, as long as there is no need to change the shelf spacing in the future.

FITTING ADJUSTABLE SHELVING

There are many different patterns of adjustable shelving on the market, with uprights and brackets usually of metal but occasionally of wood. All operate on broadly the same principle. Start by deciding on the position and spacing of the uprights; this will depend on what sort of shelf material is used, what load it will carry and what is to be stored there. Then hang the uprights on the wall, making sure that they are perfectly vertical and set level with each other. Finally, clip in the brackets and fit the shelves.

Adjustable shelves may also be wanted inside a storage unit. There are two options. The first involves drilling a series of carefully aligned holes in each side of the unit then inserting small plastic or metal shelf support studs. The second uses what is known as bookcase strip – a metal moulding with slots into which small pegs or tongues are fitted to support the shelves. Two strips are needed at each side of the unit.

PUTTING UP ADJUSTABLE SHELVES

1 Decide where to position the shelves, then fix the first upright to the wall by driving a screw through the topmost hole. Do not tighten it fully.

2 Hold a spirit level alongside the upright and pivot it until the upright is vertical. Mark the position of all the other fixing holes on the wall.

3 Swing the upright aside and drill the rest of the holes. Fit wall plugs for masonry wall fixings if needed, and drive in the remaining screws.

4 Use a spirit level to make a mark on the wall, level with the top of the first upright and at the required distance from it. Fix the second upright there.

PLANNING SHELVES

Think of how to make best use of the new storage area. It is a good idea to make a rough sketch of the plans, in order to take account of things like the height of books or record sleeves, or the clearance that ornaments or photographs will require. Aim to keep everyday items within easy reach – in practice, between about 750 mm (2 ft 6 in) and 1.5 m (5 ft) above the floor. Position deep shelves near the bottom so that it is easy to see and reach the back. Allow 25–50 mm (1–2 in) of clearance on top of the height of objects to be stored, so that they are easy to take down and put back.

Think about weight too. If the shelves will store heavy objects, the shelving material must be chosen with care, since thin shelves will sag if heavily laden unless they are well supported. With 12 mm (½ in) chipboard (particle board) and readymade veneered or melamine-faced shelves, space brackets at 450 mm (18 in) for heavy loads or 600 mm (2 ft) for light loads. With 19 mm (¾ in) chipboard or 12 mm (½ in) plywood, increase the spacing to 600 mm (2 ft) and 750 mm (2 ft 6 in) respectively. For 19 mm (¾ in) plywood, blockboard, MDF (medium-density fibreboard) or natural wood, the bracket spacing can be 750 mm (2 ft 6 in) for heavy loads, 900 mm (3 ft) for light ones.

5 Mark the upright positions on the rear edge of each shelf. Align the back of each bracket with the edge of the shelf and with the mark, and screw it on.

6 If the shelves are to fit flush against the wall, cut notches at the upright positions to fit around them and then attach the brackets as shown.

7 Position all the shelf brackets. Simply insert their tongues into the slots in the uprights. The weight of the shelf will lock them in place. Adjust the shelf spacings as wished.

USING BOOKCASE STRIP

1 Mark the positions of the top ends of the strips to ensure that they are level, then mark the screw positions to a true vertical and screw on the strips.

2 Insert pairs of pegs into the strip at each shelf position, checking that their lugs are properly engaged in the slots. Then lift the shelf into place.

USING SHELF SUPPORTS

1 Use a simple pre-drilled jig to make the holes for the shelf supports in the sides of the unit. A depth stop avoids drilling too deep.

2 Drill two sets of holes in each side of the unit, with the top of the jig held against the top of the unit to guarantee alignment. Insert the supports.

FREESTANDING SHELVING

Freestanding shelf units have several advantages over wall-mounted or built-in ones. They can easily be moved if the room layout is changed. They can be moved away from the wall to allow painting or papering. They can even be taken along when moving house. However, they have drawbacks too. Some manufactured shelving and display units are rather flimsy, and may twist out of square or sag if they are heavily loaded. In general, better results come from building units from stronger materials such as natural wood and plywood. The other problem is getting them to stand upright against the wall; skirtings (baseboards) prevent standard units from being pushed back flush with the wall surface, and carpet gripper strips make them lean forwards slightly. The answer is to design the side supports on the cantilever principle with just one point of contact with the floor, as far as possible from the wall, so that the unit presses more firmly against the wall as the load on the shelves is increased.

Since a shelf unit is basically a box with internal dividers, it can be constructed in several different ways, using simple butt joints or more complicated housings. Perhaps the best compromise between strength and ease of construction is to use glued butt joints reinforced with hardwood dowels, which give the joints the extra rigidity they need in a unit of this sort.

Start by deciding on the dimensions of the unit, then select materials to suit the likely loading the shelves will have to support. Mark up and cut matching groups of components to length in batches to ensure that they are all precisely the same size. Pre-drill all the dowel holes, using a drill stand and depth stop for holes in the board faces and a dowelling jig for those in the board ends. Insert the dowels and make up the joints. A thin plywood or hardboard backing panel can be nailed on to give the unit extra rigidity.

1 Clamp groups of identical components together. Mark them to length and cut them in one operation to ensure that they are all the same length.

2 Mark the positions of the shelf dowel holes on the unit sides, ensuring that they match. Drill them all to the required depth, using a drill stand if possible.

3 Use a dowelling jig to drill the dowel holes in the shelf ends. This ensures that the holes are correctly positioned and centred, and are drilled straight.

4 Glue the dowels and tap them into the holes in the shelf ends. Check that they all project by the same amount, and cut down any that are overlong.

5 Assemble the unit by gluing one end of each of the three shelves and joining them to one of the side panels. Then glue the other ends and add the second side panel.

6 Cut a hardboard or plywood backing panel. Check that it is perfectly square, then pin it to the back of the unit.

BELOW Freestanding shelves combined with cupboards (cabinets) and an office area offer valuable storage potential. The natural wood finish harmonizes with the decor and handsome beech wood-strip flooring.

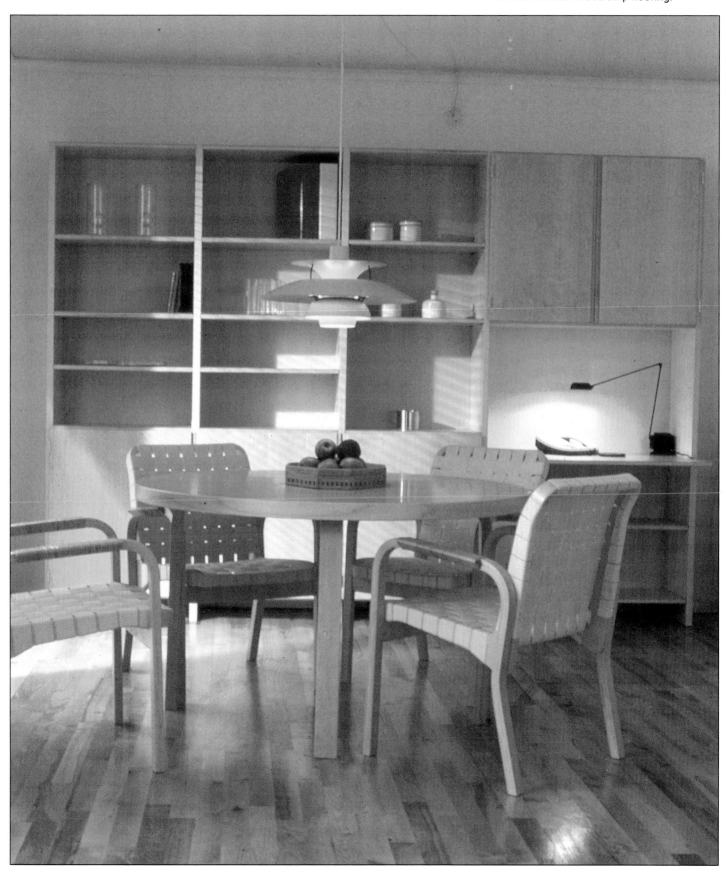

FITTING SHELVES IN ALCOVES

Alcoves beside chimney breasts (fireplace projections) or other obstructions make a perfect site for shelves, since the back and side walls can be used as supports. Although it is easy to use fixed shelf brackets or an adjustable shelving system to support shelves here, it is cheaper to fix slim wood or metal support strips directly to the alcove walls and rest the shelves on these.

If using wooden supports, cut their front ends at an angle so that they are less noticeable when the shelves are fitted. Paint them the same colour as the walls (or to tone with the wall covering) to make them even less obtrusive. If using L-shaped metal strips for the supports, choose a size that matches the shelf thickness so they are almost invisible once the shelves have been fitted.

The actual job is quite simple. Mark the shelf level on the alcove walls, cut the supports to the required lengths and screw them to the walls. Then cut your shelf to size and slip it into place, resting on the supports. It can be nailed, screwed or glued in place for extra stability. The only difficult part is in making the shelf a good fit, since the alcove walls may not be truly square. Accurate measuring of the alcove width at front and back, plus some careful scribing of the rear edge of the shelf, will ensure good results.

1 Decide on the shelf positions, then use a spirit level to mark the position of the first shelf support on one alcove wall.

2 Drill clearance and countersink holes in the supports, and use the first one to mark the fixing hole positions on the wall. Drill the holes and fix this support.

3 Rest a shelf on the first support, get it level and mark the shelf position on the opposite wall of the alcove. Then prepare the second shelf support.

4 Screw the second support in place after using it as in step 2 to mark the positions of the fixing holes on the wall. Check again that it is level.

5 Make up a set of pinch rods from scrap wood, held together as shown with a rubber band. Extend the rods to span the rear wall of the alcove.

6 Lift the rods out carefully without disturbing their positions and lay them on the rear edge of the shelf. Mark the width of the alcove on it.

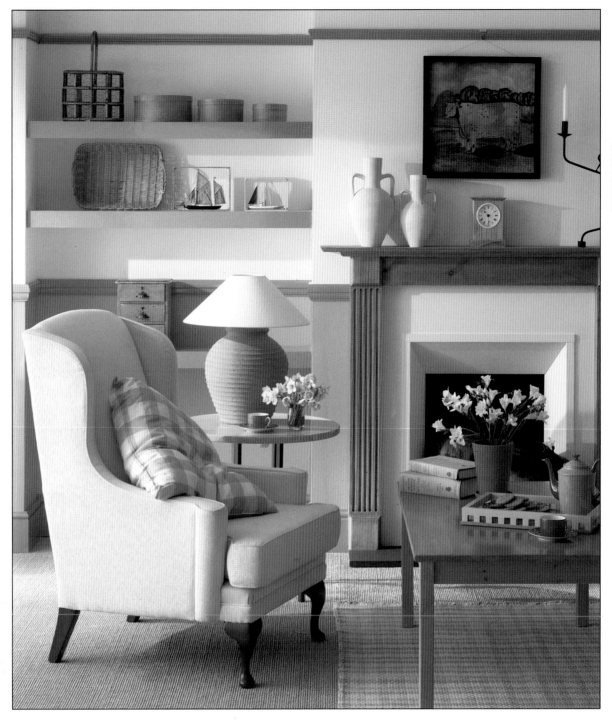

RIGHT Alcove shelving can be put to practical or decorative use. Here, painted shelves form a focal point in the room for the display of wooden boxes and wicker baskets.

7 Repeat the operation in step 5 to measure the width at the point where the front edge of the shelf will be, then transfer the measurement to the shelf.

8 Cut the shelf to width and lay it on the supports. If the fit is poor against the back wall, use a block and pencil to scribe the wall outline on it.

9 Saw carefully along the scribed line with a power jigsaw (saber saw). Sand the cut edge smooth and then fit the shelf back in position.

MAINTENANCE AND REPAIRS

Creating a well-appointed home is a thoroughly satisfying leisure activity pursued by millions of householders. Unfortunately, being creative is not the whole story; houses, like anything else, develop faults from time to time and need some attention to keep them in good working order. This final chapter looks at some of the everyday maintenance and repair problems which may occur in the home, and also explains how to use the right products – adhesives, mastics, fillers, repair tapes and fixing devices – to get good results.

OPPOSITE Keeping track of running repairs are necessary tasks for the homeowner. Shown here, from left to right and top to bottom: applying flashing tape; fixing insulation tape around doorways; removing window beads; repairing wallpaper blisters; sealing cracks with mastic; laying roof insulation; insulating sash windows; insulating pipework; and repairing stairs.

MAKING FIRM FIXINGS

Before making fixings into solid masonry, make a couple of test drillings to find out whether the wall is built of brick or lightweight blocks. If brick is identified from red or yellow bore dust, use ordinary plastic wall plugs; but if grey dust suggests lightweight blocks it is better to use a proprietary block plug which is fatter and has larger 'wings' to grip the softer material. In either case the screw must be long enough to penetrate at least 38 mm (1½ in) into the masonry behind the plaster, so use screws at least 62 mm (2½ in) long. Increase this to 75 mm (3 in) for fixings that will carry heavy loads. Screw gauge 8 will be adequate for normal loads; increase this to gauge 10 for 75 mm (3 in) screws. Make sure, too, that the screw and wall plug sizes are compatible, and take care to drill the holes at right angles to the wall surface, deep enough to accept the screw length.

Making fixings to stud (dry) walls poses different fixing problems. Cavity fixing devices such as spring or gravity toggles and cavity anchors can be used only for fixings that will carry the lightest loads. For any other use, the fixing must be made either to a horizontal nogging (cross bridging) fixed between adjacent studs – difficult to fit except during construction of the wall framework – or directly to the vertical studs themselves. These will have to be located with an electronic stud finder or, less satisfactorily, by tapping and test drilling – they are usually at 400 mm (16 in) or 600 mm (24 in) centres. Make sure that pilot holes are drilled into the centre of the stud, not near its edge, since this could result in a weak fixing. Use screws 50 mm (2 in) long for medium loads, 75 mm (3 in) long for heavy ones.

MAINTENANCE AND REPAIRS

MAKING FIXINGS IN MASONRY

1 Mark where the fixing is to go and use a masonry drill sized to match the wall plug. Wind some tape around the drill bit to act as a depth guide.

2 If the drill has an adjustable depth stop attachment, use it instead of the tape flag to set the drilling depth. Drill until the stop touches the wall surface.

MAKING FIXINGS IN PLASTERBOARD (GYPSUM BOARD)

1 If the fixing must be between joists or studs rather than into them, drill a clearance hole for the fixing device through the plasterboard.

2 Push a cavity anchor into the hole so it can expand against the back of the board, and drive in the screw. With toggles, thread the screw through the object first.

3 Choose a wall plug sized to match the screw being used, and push it into the hole until its rim is flush with the wall. Tap it with a hammer if necessary.

4 Thread the screw through a clearance hole drilled in the object being fixed, insert it in the mouth of the wall plug and drive it home.

5 Alternatively, use long-sleeved frame plugs. Drill holes through the wood and into the wall, insert the plug and tighten the screw to make the fixing.

MAKING FIXINGS INTO STUDS

1 Use an electronic stud finder to locate the stud or ceiling joist positions. It works by detecting the nails which secure the plasterboard (gypsum board).

2 When the stud or joist positions are marked, drill clearance holes in the object to be fixed at matching centres. Check these for accuracy.

3 Drill pilot holes through the board surface and into the stud or joist. Make sure that the drill bit is at right angles to the surface.

4 Insert screws in all the clearance holes, then offer up the object, align it with the pre-drilled holes and drive the screws home.

ADHESIVES, MASTICS AND REPAIR TAPES

There is a huge range of adhesives available nowadays. Their labelling is now generally much clearer than it was a few years ago, so finding the right product is considerably easier than it used to be. Here is a guide to the types that are likely to be needed for most repair jobs.

General-purpose adhesives

These are clear solvent-based adhesives which will stick paper and cardboard, wood, leather and a few types of plastic such as solid polystyrene and ABS. They are used straight from the tube. Check the instructions carefully; some recommend applying the adhesive to both surfaces, others to just one. Whichever method is used, hold or clamp the repair for a while; the adhesive takes some time after assembly to gain full strength. The joint is generally not heat-resistant and may not be water-resistant either. Adhesive can be removed from fingers, or anywhere else it gets by mistake, with cellulose thinner, acetone or nail varnish remover – but the last will attack gloss paint, french polish, some varnishes, and any plastic that the adhesive will stick.

Adhesives for wood

The most widely used type of adhesive for general woodwork is *PVA woodworking adhesive*, often referred to as 'white glue'. It will bond softwood, hardwood and all manufactured boards, and is colourless when dry; spills can be wiped away with a damp cloth before the adhesive sets. The joint must be clamped until the adhesive hardens – for a couple of hours at least – to get the best results. Exposure to damp will weaken the adhesive and cause failure. If such exposure is likely, be sure to use one of the cross-linking versions which give a high degree of water resistance.

Adhesives for laminates

Plastic laminates, flexible sheet materials such as foam and leather, and vinyl or cork floor tiles are stuck in place with a *contact adhesive*. This is spread on both surfaces and is allowed to become touch-dry before the two are pressed together. The resulting bond is instant, and cannot normally be repositioned; but some kinds offer a degree of slip – they are often called *thixotropic adhesives*. Contact adhesive is also moderately heatproof and water-resistant.

Most contact adhesives are solvent-based, and the fumes are both inflammable and noxious to inhale, so work with good ventilation and no naked lights. Clean up spills with the manufacturer's own solvent, cellulose thinner, acetone or nail varnish remover. Water-based contact adhesives are also available, and these are much safer and more pleasant to use; spills can be removed while still wet with a damp cloth.

Adhesives for plastics

Some plastics are very difficult to stick with adhesives. Two which cannot be stuck by any means are polythene (polyethylene) and polypropylene, the bendy plastics used for such things as washing-up bowls (wash bowls) and buckets; they must be fused by heat. Flexible PVC – used for seat covers, sunbeds and beach balls, for example – can be stuck with special *vinyl repair adhesive*. *Polystyrene cement* or general-purpose adhesive will mend rigid polystyrene – used for some kitchen and bathroom accessories – and the similar but tougher ABS. Do not use it for expanded polystyrene ceiling tiles or coving (crown molding), though, as

SILICONE MASTIC Use silicone mastic to seal around bathroom fittings. Push the nozzle along the gap so it leaves a neat concave finish to the mastic bead.

ACRYLIC MASTIC Use acrylic mastic indoors and frame sealant outdoors to seal gaps between wood and masonry where a rigid filler would tend to crack and fall out.

REPAIR TAPE Use repair tapes to make temporary repairs to cracked glass, or to waterproof glazing bars on glass roofs. Simply press the tape into place.

the adhesive will eat these away. Always use a special adhesive paste made for the purpose.

For other plastics, experiment with epoxy resin adhesives, two-part acrylics or cyanoacrylates (see right).

Mastics and repair tapes

Mastic is a permanently flexible adhesive filler that is used to seal joints indoors and outdoors. The material comes in cartridges, and is usually extruded by using a hand-held gun. The resulting bead of mastic is simply piped into place, and may be smoothed out with a wet finger or a filling knife (putty knife) if necessary. Various types are available: *acrylic* types are used as a general-purpose decorating filler indoors; *silicone* types are best for such jobs as waterproofing joints around bathroom and kitchen fittings; and *frame sealants* are designed for filling and sealing gaps around window and door frames.

Repair tapes of various types are used to make temporary repairs to things such as cracked glass, leaky glazing bars and porous flashings. As with mastics, choose the type appropriate to the task in hand.

Adhesives for glass, china and metal

Three types of adhesive can be used for repairing these materials. Each has advantages and disadvantages.

Epoxy resin adhesives are two-part products, prepared by mixing equal quantities of resin and hardener, and generally applied to both surfaces. Quick-setting types set hard in a few minutes, others take about half an hour, with full bond strength developing more slowly. Once set, the bond is heat- and waterproof, and the adhesive will fill gaps; however, it does leave a noticeable glue line, and this may darken with time. Clean up spills with white spirit (paint thinner) or methylated spirit (wood alcohol), and trim off dried adhesive with a sharp utility knife.

Cyanoacrylate adhesives, also known as superglues, are liquids which are applied sparingly to just one surface. The resulting glue line is very thin, so they are ideal for repairing china and glass, but apart from the newer gel types the adhesive has negligible gap-filling properties so the parts must be a good fit. With most brands, the joint is not waterproof, but some are specially

formulated for repairing items that will have to be washed or must hold liquids. Avoid skin contact when using this type of adhesive; if fingers, or anything else, get stuck together, instantly immerse them in hot soapy water and gently peel the stuck areas apart. Some manufacturers supply a special release agent with the adhesive. Always keep glues away from children, but especially this type.

Two-part acrylic adhesives are not mixed directly; instead adhesive is applied to one surface and hardener to the other, and the two brought together to form the bond. This sticks immediately, and reaches full strength in a few hours. The adhesive has good heat resistance and is fairly waterproof, but does not fill gaps very well. Wipe up spills with a dry cloth or use methylated spirits. Alternatively, trim off dried adhesive with a sharp knife.

Speciality adhesives

The shelves of a do-it-yourself store will also contain all kinds of special-purpose adhesives, clearly labelled as to their use. These include *wallpaper paste*, *ceramic tile adhesive* and *coving (crown molding) adhesive*.

1 **FLASHING TAPE** Use flashing tape to seal porous felt or metal flashings. Start by brushing on a coat of special primer; use an old paintbrush and wear protective gloves.

2 Unroll the flashing tape, peel off the release paper and press the strip into position over the band of primer, bedding it well into the roof/wall angle.

3 To ensure that the tape bonds well to the wall and roof surfaces, run a wallpaper seam roller firmly along both edges of the strip.

CURING DOOR PROBLEMS

A well fitted door should have a long and trouble-free life. If it does misbehave, the problem is generally the door binding against its frame and, in extreme cases, failing to shut properly. There is likely to be one of three causes: a build-up of paint on the door and frame surfaces after years of repainting, expansion due to atmospheric conditions – the door sticks in damp weather as moisture causes it to swell slightly, but it shrinks and closes freely in dry weather – and hinge faults caused either by wear and tear or bad fitting.

Where a paint build-up is to blame, the remedy is quite simple; strip off the old paint from the door edge back to bare wood, and repaint from scratch.

If atmospheric conditions are to blame, the solution is to plane down the door edges slightly to increase the clearance between door and frame. The door will have to be taken off its hinges to do this unless it is only the leading edge that is binding.

Hinge faults that can cause binding include hinge screws standing proud or working loose, and hinge recesses being cut too deep or too shallow. In each case the cure is relatively simple; the biggest problem is often trying to undo the old hinge screws, especially if they have become encrusted with paint over the years. Clean out the slots in the screw heads thoroughly before trying to remove the screws; paint remover is useful for this. Then position the screwdriver in the slot and give the handle a sharp blow with a hammer to help free the grip of the threads in the wood.

1 If the hinge screws show signs of pulling out, remove them, drill out the screw holes and hammer in glued dowels. Then drill new pilot holes.

2 If the door is striking the frame because it has expanded, close it and mark a pencil line on the door face against the edge of the frame.

5 If the door binds on the hinge side of the frame, the hinge recesses may be too deep. Remove the hinge and pin some packing into the recess.

6 Drill fresh pilot holes for the screws through the packing piece, and drive the fixing screws back into place. Make sure their heads fit in the countersinks.

MAINTENANCE AND REPAIRS

3 Take the door off its hinges, remove the handles and latch mechanism, and plane the leading edge of the door down until the pencil line has disappeared.

4 If the door is binding at the top or bottom, take this opportunity to plane off a little wood there too. Plane inwards from the corners to avoid causing splits.

7 Alternatively, relocate the hinges in a new position. Chisel out the new recesses and refit the hinge.

8 If the hinge recesses are too shallow the hinge leaves will bind and stop the door from closing. Remove the hinges and chisel out the recesses slightly.

CURING WINDOW PROBLEMS

By far the commonest window problem is a cracked or broken pane, caused by a flying object or by the window being allowed to slam. Make a temporary repair to cracked glass with a clear waterproof repair tape – not household adhesive tape – but aim to replace the pane at the earliest opportunity. If the glass is broken, lift out all the loose pieces for safety's sake and make a temporary repair by fixing heavy-duty polythene (polyethylene) sheet or a piece of board over the opening.

When measuring up for the replacement glass, measure all four sides in case the rebate in the frame is not perfectly square, and use the smaller of each pair of figures. Subtract 3 mm (⅛ in) from each one to allow for clearance all around, and note which way the pattern ran if the glass was obscured rather than clear. Take a piece of patterned glass when buying a replacement so as to be sure of getting the correct type.

The other problems that windows suffer from are similar to those affecting doors – paint build-up, expansion or warping. They may also pull out of square if the frame corner joints start to open up, causing the casement to bind in its frame and possibly also cracking the glass. The trouble can be cured by strengthening the frame corners with small L-shaped metal repair plates; cut shallow recesses for them and disguise their presence with filler and a coat or two of paint.

TIP

Always dispose of broken glass safely, by wrapping it in newspaper and then packing it in a box so it cannot injure anyone.

REPLACING BROKEN GLASS

1 When a window breaks, remove all the loose glass immediately for safety's sake. Wear stout gloves to protect hands and dispose of the glass safely.

2 Use an old chisel or a glazier's knife to remove all the old putty from the rebate in the frame. Take care not to cut into the wood while doing this.

3 Use a pair of pincers or pliers to pull out the old glazing sprigs all around the frame. Metal frames have glazing clips; save these and reuse them.

4 Knead some putty with the hands to warm and soften it, then press it into the rebate by extruding it between thumb and forefinger.

5 Set the replacement pane in position against the bedding putty with equal clearance all around, and press it into place around the edges to compress the putty.

6 Secure the pane in the rebate by tapping in glazing sprigs at roughly 300 mm (12 in) intervals. Replace clips in their locating holes in metal frames.

7 Repeat step 4 to extrude a bead of facing putty all around the pane, then neaten it to a 45° bevel by drawing the blade of a putty knife along it.

8 Trim off excess putty from the outside and inside of the pane and leave it to harden for about 14 days before painting over it to disguise and seal the joints.

CURING BINDING CASEMENTS

1 If a build-up of paint is causing the edge of the casement to bind against the frame, strip it back to bare wood. Use chemical strippers; heat may crack the glass.

2 If the frame has swollen because of moisture penetration, plane a little wood off the leading edge. Prime and paint it immediately to keep the wood dry.

3 If the corner joints of a casement show signs of opening up and the frame is pulling out of square, screw on small L-shaped metal repair plates.

PATCHING WALL AND CEILING DAMAGE

Plasterboard (gypsum board) is an immensely versatile material for lining walls and ceilings, since it provides a smooth surface for any finish and has useful sound-deadening and fireproofing properties. The one thing it does not do very well is to resist impacts, and the resulting hole cannot simply be patched with filler because the board's strength has been lost at the point of damage. The solution is either to strengthen the board or to replace a section altogether.

Very small holes can be disguised with self-adhesive scrim tape and cellulose filler (spackle), but holes more than about 50 mm (2 in) across need a more substantial repair. Use an offcut of plasterboard and cut a piece slightly narrower than the hole width and twice as long as its height to use as a patch. Pierce a hole in it, thread a piece of string through, tie one end to a nail and pull this against the face of the patch. Then butter some plaster or filler onto the other face of the patch and push it into the hole, keeping hold of the string with the other hand. Position the patch against the inner face of the plasterboard, pulling on the string to help the filler stick it in place. When it has stuck fast, fill the hole and cut off the string.

For larger holes – a foot through the ceiling, for example – in plasterboard and (in older properties) lath-and-plaster surfaces, the only solution is to cut out the damaged piece and nail on a new section in its place. Supports will need to be fixed around the edges of the opening where the damaged section has been cut out. Then fill the cut edges, apply joint tape to hide them and skim over the patch with a little plaster to complete the repair.

PATCHING SMALL HOLES IN PLASTERBOARD (GYPSUM BOARD)

1 Cut a plasterboard patch slightly longer and narrower than the hole, and thread a length of string with a nail tied on through a hole in its centre.

2 Butter some plaster or filler onto the edges of the patch and feed it end-on into the hole, keeping hold of the string with the other hand.

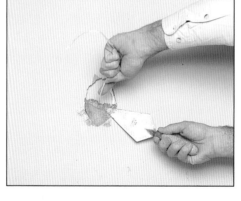

3 Pull the string to hold the patch against the rear face of the board, then fill the recess with plaster or filler and cut off the string.

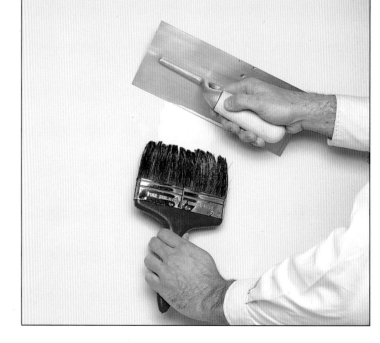

4 Complete the repair by applying a skim coat of plaster over the patch. Flick water onto it with a brush and polish it smooth with a float.

PATCHING LARGER HOLES IN PLASTERBOARD (GYPSUM BOARD)

1 If the plasterboard surface is more extensively damaged, cut through it with a sharp knife back to the adjacent wall studs or ceiling joists.

2 Cut across to the stud or joist centres, then make two vertical cuts down the centre of the stud or joist to free the damaged panel.

3 Cut two strips of wood to fit between the studs/joists, and screw or nail them into place so they will support the edges of the main board and the patch.

4 Cut a plasterboard patch to match the section removed, and nail it into place. Fill and tape the joints and skim plaster over the repair to conceal it.

REPAIRING LATH-AND-PLASTER SURFACES

1 If the wood laths are split or broken, pull them away from the surface. Remove any loose sections of plaster from around the site of the damage.

2 Continue cutting back the old plaster and the laths behind it to expose the studs or ceiling joists at each side of the hole. Square off the edges.

3 Cut a plasterboard patch to fit the hole, and nail it in place. Add two support strips as described for patching plasterboard if the panel is large.

4 Complete the repair by plastering over the patch after filling and taping the cut edges all around. Polish the repair with a steel float.

CURING FLOOR PROBLEMS

Floorboards suffer more from being lifted for access to pipes and cables beneath them than they do from everyday wear and tear. If the floor has nothing worse than the occasional creak, the trouble can generally be cured by lifting floor coverings and then nailing – or better still, screwing – the offending board down again. With a chipboard (particle board) floor, make sure that the boards are nailed to every joist they cross, not just at the edges; if they are not, the boards can bow upwards and will then bang against the joists when walked on.

Before lifting a section of floor to gain access to services below it, look first of all to see whether someone has already cut an access panel. If they have not, it will be necessary to create one. Locate the joist position closest to where access is needed – the flooring nail positions will reveal its whereabouts. Then drill a starter hole and use a jigsaw (saber saw) to make a 45° cut next to the joist. Prise up the cut end and wedge a strip of wood underneath it, then saw through the board over the centre of the next joist to free the section. To replace it, nail one end to the joist and either skew nail (toe nail) the other angled end to its neighbour or nail a support block to the side of the joist and nail or screw the board end to that.

With concrete floors, the only repair that is likely to be needed is the filling of cracks or small potholes that may be revealed when an old floor covering is lifted. Cut back any loose edges, brush away loose material and fill the cracks with a fine mortar mix. If the floor surface is sound but uneven or out of level, lay a self-smoothing compound over it.

CREATING AN ACCESS PANEL

1 Start by locating an adjacent joist. Drill a starter hole for the saw blade. Cut through the board at 45° next to the joist with a jigsaw (saber saw).

2 Use a bolster (stonecutter's chisel) or a similar broad-bladed levering tool to prise up the cut end of the board and release its fixing nails.

3 Slide a length of scrap wood under the raised end of the board to hold it clear of the floor, and saw through it above the centre of the next joist.

4 To replace the panel, simply lay it back in position. Nail the square-cut end to its joist and skew nail (toe nail) the angled end to the neighbouring board.

5 An alternative way of supporting the cut ends of an access panel is to nail small wood blocks to each side of the adjacent joists.

6 The panel can also be screwed down onto the wooden blocks. This will allow easy access without damaging the panel.

REPAIRING A CONCRETE FLOOR

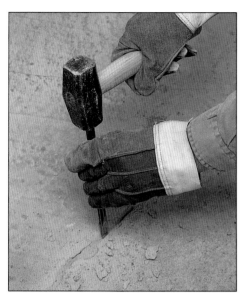

1 If cracks are found in a concrete floor after lifting old floor coverings, use a cold (box) chisel and club (spalling) hammer to undercut the edges of the crack.

2 Brush away all loose material from the crack, then use the crevice nozzle of a vacuum cleaner to remove dust which the brush will not pick up.

3 Dilute some PVA building (white general purpose) adhesive as recommended on the can, and brush it along the surface of the crack to help the repair mortar to bond to it.

4 Mix up some quick-setting repair mortar and trowel it into the crack, levelling it flush with the surrounding concrete. Leave it to harden.

5 If the floor has noticeable potholes in its surface, pack the hole with small pieces of stone or other non-compressible filler.

6 Patch the pothole with quick-setting mortar, using the edge of the steel float to remove excess mortar so the patch is flush with its surroundings.

REPAIRING WALL COVERINGS

It is a simple matter to repair minor damage to painted walls and ceilings and then to cover it up with a fresh coat of paint. With wall coverings, patching damage or curing paperhanging defects requires a different approach.

The commonest form of damage to a wall covering is an impact that leaves a jagged tear. If the torn part is still attached, brush some paste onto its rear face and press it back into place, rolling it flat with a seam roller.

If the torn part is missing it will be necessary to patch the damage. If there are some offcuts from the original papering job, cut a patch from them. If not, cut and dry-strip a patch from an out-of-sight area behind a piece of furniture to use for the repair. Tear around the edges of the patch, holding it face down, to create a thin 'feathered' edge, then paste it, place it over the damaged area and flatten it with a seam roller. If the paper is a thick two-layer duplex type, try to peel away the backing paper to reduce the thickness of the patch.

Two other common problems, blisters and lifting seams, are the result of inadequate pasting during paperhanging. It is a relatively simple task to slit blisters open and lift dry seams to apply a little fresh paste and stick the covering firmly back to the wall. With fragile printed or flocked wall coverings, take care not to get paste on the surface.

PATCHING DAMAGED WALLPAPER

1 Cut a repair patch from an offcut of the original wall covering, or strip one from behind a piece of furniture. Check that it will cover the damage and match the pattern.

CURING DRY BLISTERS

1 If a dry blister appears after wallpapering, use a sharp utility knife to make two cuts through it at right angles.

2 Peel back the triangular tongues formed and apply a little paste to the wall surface and to the back of the tongues. Leave to soak for a few minutes.

3 Press the triangles back into place and run a seam roller along the cuts to bond the paper firmly to the wall and leave an almost invisible repair.

2 **ABOVE** Carefully tear along the edges of the patch to reduce its thickness and create a thin feathered edge. Check that no backing paper is visible.

3 **BELOW** Some two-layer duplex papers are too thick to use as a patch. Try to separate the backing paper at a corner of the patch and peel it off.

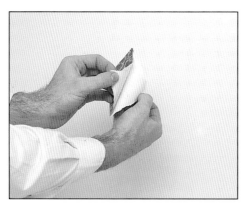

4 **BELOW** Paste the back of the patch and place it over the damaged area, aligning the pattern carefully. Then 'iron' it into place with a seam roller.

STICKING DRY SEAMS

1 If a seam has failed to stick flat, lift it with a filling knife (putty knife) and use a slip of abrasive paper to sand off the dried paste behind it.

2 Use the filling knife to hold the edge of the wall covering away from the wall, and brush a little paste onto the back and the wall surface. Leave to soak.

3 Press the seam down flat with a seam roller, then use a sponge or damp cloth to remove any paste that has oozed onto the face of the wall covering.

MANUFACTURERS AND SUPPLIERS

Most of the manufacturers listed here supply their products to good independent retailers, major stores and DIY multiples. Try your local outlets first; they will usually be able to help you and can be found in the area business directory. If you have difficulties in obtaining specific items, contact the relevant company head office for more information.

TOOLS AND BASIC MATERIALS

Black & Decker Ltd *Power tools* Westpoint, The Grove, Slough, Berkshire SL1 1QQ, UK. 0753 511234

General Woodwork Supplies (SN) Ltd *Timber, tools and hardware* 76–80 Stoke Newington High St, London N16 5BR, UK. 071-254 6052

Gripperrods plc *Carpeting tools and accessories* Wyrley Brook Park, Walkmill Lane, Bridgtown, Cannock, Staffordshire WS11 3XA, UK. 0922 417777

Hobbs & Co Ltd *Builders Merchants* 88

Blackfriars Road, London SE1 8HA, UK. 071-928 1891

Mosley Stone *Painting and decorating tools* Wellington Road, Leeds LS12 1DU, UK. 0532 630221

Plasplugs Ltd *Tiling tools* Wetmore Road, Burton-on-Trent, Staffordshire DE14 1SD, UK. 0283 30303

Stanley Tools *Woodworking, Painting and decorating tools* Woodside, Sheffield S3 9PD, UK. 0742 768888

Whincop & Son Ltd *Timber and builders merchants* 32/40 Stoke Newington Church St, London N16 0LU, UK. 071-254 5044

Allway Tools Inc *Hand tools* 1255 Seabury Avenue, Bronx, New York, New York 10462, USA. (212) 792 3636

Black & Decker *Power tools* Communications Department, 702 East Joppa Road, Towson, Maryland 21286, USA

Robert Bosch Power Tool Corporation *Power Tools* 100 Bosch Blvd, New Bern, North Carolina 28562, USA

Home Building & Lumber Co Inc *Lumber* 1621 Ave H, Rosenberg, Texas 77471, USA. (713) 342 4282

Skil Corporation *Tools* 4300 West Peterson Avenue, Chicago, Illinois 60646, USA

Stanley Tools *Woodworking, painting and decorating tools*

1000 Stanley Drive, New Britain, Connecticut 06053, USA

Seco Tools Canada Inc *Hand tools* Mississanga, Ontario, Canada. (416) 568 4080

Parburyss Building Products *Wood merchants* 30 Bando Road, Springvale, Victoria 3171, Australia. (03) 547 9033

H J Reece Pty Ltd *Hand tools* 2 Barney Street, North Parramatta, NSW 2151, Australia. 008 01 8606 (toll free)

Stanley Works Pty Ltd *Woodworking, painting and decorating tools* PO Box 10, 400 Whitehorse Road, Nunawading, Victoria 3131, Australia

Wreckair Pty Ltd *Power tools* 2 Chisholm Road, Regents Park,

NSW 2143, Australia. (02) 645 4000

Nees Hardware Ltd *Tools* 11–15 Pretoria Street, Lower Hutt, New Zealand

Stanley Tools (NZ) Ltd *Woodworking, painting and decorating tools* PO Box 12-582, Penrose, Auckland, New Zealand

Tuf Tools CC *Woodworking, painting and decorating tools* PO Box 212, Maraisburg 1700, Transvaal, South Africa

PAINTS & WOOD FINISHES

Laura Ashley Ltd 150 Bath Road, Maidenhead, Berkshire SL6 4YS, UK. 0628 770345

Cuprinol Ltd Adderwell, Frome, Somerset BA11 1NL, UK. 0373 465151

Crown Paints Crown House, Hollins Road, Darwen, Lancs BB3 0BG, UK. 0254 704951

Dulux (ICI plc Paints Division) Wexham Road, Slough, Berkshire SL2 5DS, UK. 0753 550000

Arthur Sanderson & Sons Ltd 100 Acres, Oxford Road, Uxbridge, Middx UB8 1HY, UK. 0895 238244

Builders Square Inc *Decorating store* 9725 Datapoint Drive, San Antonio, Texas 78229, USA. (512) 616 8000

Wilson W A & Sons Inc *Decorating store* 6 Industrial Park Drive, Wheeling, WV 26003, USA. (304) 232 2200

Dulux Australia 145 Cabarita Road, Concord, NSW 23137, Australia. (02) 736 5111

Pascol Paints Australia Pty Ltd PO Box 63, Rosebery, NSW 2018, Australia. (02) 669 2266

Sikkens (Tenaru Pty Ltd) PO Box 768, Darlinghurst, Sydney, NSW 2010, Australia. (02) 357 4500

Taubmans 51 McIntyre Road, Sunshine, Victoria 3020, Australia. (03) 311 0211

ICI Hutt Park Road, PO Box 30749, Lower Hutt, New Zealand

Taubmans (New Zealand) Ltd 10 Portsmouth Road, PO Box 14064, Kilbirnie, Wellington, New Zealand. 0800 735 551 (toll free)

Dulux (Pty) Ltd 8 Juyn Street, Alrode, PO Box 123704 Alrode, South Africa

WALL COVERINGS

Laura Ashley (see *Paints*)

Crown Berger Ltd (see *Paints*)

Forbo–CP (Fablon) Ltd Station Road, Cramlington, Northumberland NE23 8AQ, UK. 0670 718300

Forbo–Kingfisher Ltd Lune Mills, Lancaster, Lancashire LA1 5QN, UK. 0524 65222

Harlequin Wallcoverings Ltd Cossington Road, Sileby, Nr Loughborough, Leicestershire LE12 7RU, UK. 0509 816575

Monkwell Fabrics and Wallpapers 10–12 Wharfdale Road, Bournemouth, Dorset BH4 9BT, UK. 0202 752944

Arthur Sanderson & Sons Ltd (see *Paints*)

Muriel Short Designs Hewitts Estate, Elmbridge Road, Cranley, Surrey GU6 8LW, UK. 0483 271211

Today Interiors Hollis Road, Grantham, Lincolnshire NG31 7QH, UK. 0476 74401

Crown Wallcovering Corp 20 Horizon Boulevard, South Hackensack, New Jersey 07606, USA. (201) 440 7000

Mazer's Discount Home Centers Inc *Decorating store* 210 41st Street S, Birmingham, Alabama 35222, USA. (205) 591 6565

Pratt & Lambert Inc *Decorating store* 75 Tonawanda Street, Buffalo, New York 14207, USA. (716) 873 6000

North American Decorative Products Inc 1055 Clark Boulevard, Brompton, Ontario, Canada L6T 3W4

Davro Interiors 616 Hay Street, Holimont, WA 6014, Australia. (09) 387 4888

International Paints Birmingham Avenue, Villawood, NSW 2163, Australia. (02) 728 7577

TILES

The Amtico Company Ltd *Vinyl tiles* 1177 St George Street, London W1R 9DE, UK. 071-629 6258

Castelnau Tiles *Wall and floor tiles* 175 Church Road, Barnes, London SW13 9HR, UK. 081-741 2452

Corres Mexican Tiles *Ceramic wall tiles* 219–221 Chiswick High Road, London W4, UK. 081-994 0215

Fired Earth Tiles plc and **The Merchant Tiler** *Ceramic, terracotta, stone and slate tiles* Twyford Mill, Oxford Road, Adderbury, Banbury, Oxfordshire OX17 3HP, UK. 0295 812088/812179

MANUFACTURERS AND SUPPLIERS

H & R Johnson Tiles Ltd *Ceramic floor and wall tiles* Highgate Works, Tunstall, Stoke-on-Trent ST6 4JX, UK. 0782 575575

Daniel Platt Ltd *Natural clay products* Brownhill Tileries, Canal Lane, Tunstall, Stoke-on-Trent ST6

4NY, UK. 0782 577187

Westco Ltd *Vinyl, cork and wood-block floor tiles* Penarth Road, Cardiff, South Glamorgan CF1 7YN, UK. 0222 233926

Wicanders (GB) Ltd *Cork floor and wall tiles* Stoner House, Kilnmead, Crawley, West Sussex RH10 2BG, UK. 0293 527700

American Olean Tile Company 1000 Cannon Avenue, Lansdale, Pennsylvania 19446, USA. (215) 855-1111

Armstrong World Industries PO Box 3001, Lancaster, Pennsylvania 17603, USA. (800) 233-3823

Crossville Ceramics Box 1168, Crossville, Tennessee 38557, USA. (615) 484-2110

Latco Tiles 2948 Gleneden Street, Los Angeles, California 90039, USA. (213) 664-1171

Summitville Tiles Inc Box 73, Summitville, Ohio 43962, USA. (216) 223-1511

Greenbank Tertech Pty Ltd *Ceramic tiles* 5 Hereford Street, Berkeley Vale, NSW 2259, Australia. (043) 88 4522

Bruce Floor (Vic) Pty Ltd *Linoleum tiles* 60 Punt Road, Windsor, Victoria 3181, Australia. (03) 51 5222

FLOOR COVERINGS

Crucial Trading Ltd *Natural floor coverings* 4 St Barnabas Street, London SW1, UK. 071-730 0075

Forbo Nairn Ltd *Cushioned vinyl and linoleum* PO Box 1, Kirkcaldy, Fife, Scotland DY1 2SB. 0592 261111

Heuga UK Ltd *Carpet tiles* The Gate House, Gate House Way, Aylesbury, Buckinghamshire HP19 3DL, UK. 0296 393244

Junckers Ltd *Hardwood strip flooring* Wheaton Court Commercial Centre, Wheaton Road, Witham, Essex CM8 3UJ, UK. 0376 517512

Kosset Carpets Ltd Tofshaw Lane, Bradford, West Yorkshire BD4 6QW, UK. 0274 681881

Tomkinsons Carpets Ltd PO Box 11, Duke Place, Kidderminster, Worcestershire DY10 2JR, UK. 0562 820006

Westco Ltd *Wood-block floor tiles* (see Tiles)

Woodward Grosvenor & Co Ltd *Carpets* Stourvale Mills, Green Street, Kidderminster, Worcestershire DY10 2AT, UK. 0562 820020

Kentile Floors Inc 58 Second Avenue, Brooklyn, New York, New York 11215, USA

Stark Carpet Corporation 977 Third Avenue, New York, New York 10022, USA

Dorsett Carpet Mills Inc 502 11th Avenue, Dalton, Georgia 30721, USA. (706) 278 1961

ETC Carpet Mill Ltd 3100 S Susan Street, Santa Ana, California 92704, USA. (714) 546 5601

Bruce Floor (Vic) Pty Ltd *Carpets* (see Tiles)

Carpet and Decor Centre 26 Central Road, Fordsburg 2092, Johannesburg, South Africa. (011) 833 2311

FEATURES & FITTINGS

J D Beardmore & Co Ltd *Architectural hardware* 3–4 Percy Street, London W1P 0EJ, UK. 071-637 7041

Richard Burbidge Ltd *Timber mouldings, shelving and fire surrounds* Whittington

Road, Oswestry, Shropshire SY11 1HZ, UK. 0691 655131

Fireplace Designers Ltd *Fire surrounds and accessories* 157c Great Portland Street, London W1N 5FB, UK. 071-580 9893/4

Harrison Drape *Curtain poles and accessories* Bradford Street, Birmingham B12 0PE, UK. 021 766 6111

Hodkin & Jones (Sheffield) Ltd *Decorative plaster mouldings* Callywhite Lane, Dronfield, Sheffield S18 6XP, UK. 0246 290888

Fixture Hardware Co Inc 4711 N Lamon Avenue, Chicago, Illinois 60630, USA. (312) 777 6100

Handy Hardware Wholesale Inc 8300 Tewantin Drive, Houston, Texas 77061, USA. 97130 644 1495

SOFT FURNISHINGS

Laura Ashley Ltd (see Paints)

Forbo–Kingfisher Ltd (see Wall Coverings)

Harlequin wallcoverings Ltd (see Wall Coverings)

Monkwell Fabrics and Wallpapers (see Wall Coverings)

Arthur Sanderson & Sons Ltd (see Paints)

Muriel Short Designs (see Wall Coverings)

Today Interiors (see Wall Coverings)

Decor Home Fashion Inc 140 58th Street, Brooklyn, New York 11220, USA. (718) 921 1030

Southwest Quilted Products Inc 18100 Kovacs Lane, Huntington Beach, California 92648, USA. (714) 841 5656

North American Decorative Products Inc (see Wall Coverings)

Tissus Rosedale Inc D'Anjou, Quebec,

Canada. (514) 351 8402

Nichimen Australia Ltd 3rd Floor, 60–70 Elizabeth Street, Sydney, NSW 2000, Australia. (02) 223 7122

STORAGE

Addis Ltd Ware Road, Hertford, Hertfordshire SG13 7HL, UK. 0992 584221

Cliffhanger Shelving Systems 8 Fletchers Square, Temple Farm Industrial Estate, Southend-on-Sea, Essex SS2 5RN, UK. 0702 613135

MFI Southon House, 333 The Hyde, Edgware Road, Collingdale, London NW9 6TD, UK. 081-200 0200.

Silver Lynx Products Ltd Lynx House, 10/11 Amber Business Village, Amber Close, Tamworth, Staffordshire B77 4RP, UK. 0827 311888

Spur Shelving Ltd Otterspool Way, Watford, Hertfordshire WD2 8HT, UK. 0923 226071

Shelves & Cabinets Unlimited 7880 Dunbrook Road, San Diego, California 92126, USA. (619) 578 4200

Bernhard Woodworking Ltd Inc 3670 Woodhead Drive, Northbrook, Illinois 60062, USA. (708) 291 1040

Caringbah Sheet Metal (Aust) Pty Ltd 42 Cawarra Road, Caringbah, NSW 2229, Australia. (02) 524 0791

Algoran Shelvit (Pty) Ltd Botha Street, Alrode, Alberton, South Africa. (011) 640 864 3900

SUNDRIES

Concord Lighting Ltd Alton House, High Holborn, London WC1, UK. 071-497 1400

Ideal-Standard Ltd *Bathroom equipment, furniture and accessories* PO Box 60, National Avenue, Hull HU5 4JE, UK. 0482 46461

Mazda Lighting Miles Road, Mitcham, Surrey CR4 3YX, UK. 081-640 1221.

Oracstar Limited *Plumbing and ventilation products* Weddell Way, Brackmills, Northampton NN4 0HS, UK. 0604 702181

Philips Lighting Ltd PO Box 298, City House, 420/430 London Road, Croydon, Surrey CR9 3QR, UK. 081-665 6655

INDEX

The publishers would like to thank Pat Murphy for demonstrating the carpet laying sequences. Many thanks also to New Islington and Hackney Housing Association for the use of one of their properties which was awaiting repair.

In addition, the publishers would like to thank the companies listed below for their generous help in either loaning or providing materials and equipment for use in the production of this title. For more details and further addresses, see the Manufacturers and Suppliers list.

J D Beardmore & Co. Ltd
Black & Decker
Crown Paints
Forbo Nairn Ltd
General Woodwork Supplies Ltd
Gripperrods plc
Hobbs & Co. Ltd
Ideal-Standard Ltd
H & R Johnson Tiles Ltd
Junckers Ltd
Kosset Carpets Ltd
Mosley-Stone
Plasplugs Ltd
Daniel Platt Ltd
Stanley Tools
Whincop & Son Ltd

The publishers would also like to thank the following companies for their kind permission to reproduce the following pictures in the book:

t = top; b = bottom; c = centre; l = left; r = right.

Crown Paints: page 8.
Dulux: pages 2–3, 6 bl, 107.
Cristal (H & R Johnson Tiles) Ltd: page 6 br.
Crucial Trading Ltd: page 7 bc.
Fired Earth Tiles plc: page 88.
Forbo–CP (Fablon) Ltd: page 7 bl.
Forbo–Kingfisher Ltd: page 99 r.
Forbo–Nairn Ltd: page 87.
Harlequin Wallcoverings Ltd: pages 7 br, 26.
Heuga: page 81 bl br.
Junckers Ltd: pages 91, 105.
The Merchant Tiler: page 64.
MFI: page 6 bc.
Mr Tomkinson: page 70.
Sanderson: page 79.

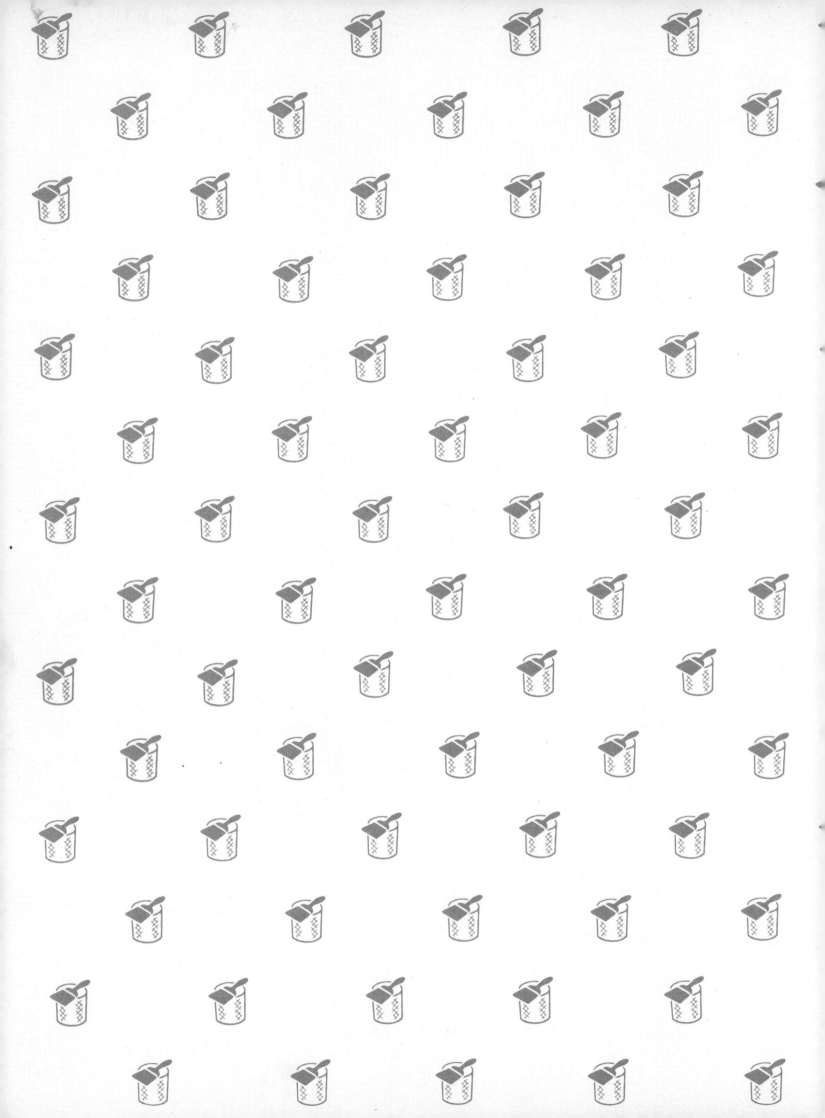